To Mary from Walter

Best wishes always,

Messages from the Interior

Messages from the Interior

A Psychiatrist's Life

Walter Turke, M.D., L.F.A.P.A

VANTAGE PRESS
New York

FIRST EDITION

Published by Vantage Press, Inc.
516 West 34th Street, New York, New York 10001

Manufactured in the United States of America
ISBN: 0-533-11528-0

Library of Congress Catalog Card No.: 95-90299

0 9 8 7 6 5 4 3 2 1

To my children:
Garrett, Tiffanie, and Cindy,
with love

A very special thank you to my friend, James R. Kesler, for his support and valuable assistance in making the dream of this book a reality . . .

Chapter 1

The Sniper was not a happy man; that was obvious as he stormed into my office, slamming the door behind him. I looked at my five fourth-year Michigan State University medical students trying to maintain their composure even though I knew their hearts were beating faster. Of course the Sniper was seldom ever happy, which is why he was my patient in the first place. Matt, whom I had privately nicknamed the Sniper, had been a young man when he was first sent to war in Korea, but he had aged rapidly while he was over there. He had been trained to kill, but not the usual ways, the kind full of swagger and glory and guts. His was the version both cowardly and brave at the same time. Isolated, he would lie hidden, stalking, bringing sudden death to an unsuspecting enemy.

As a sniper he had been one of the most decorated soldiers to come out of the Korean conflict, because he had terminated the lives of over a hundred North Koreans. In my capacity as an academic psychiatric consultant to the Veterans Administration hospital in Saginaw, Michigan, I became Matt's physician. He was unable to talk much about his pain because he had always kept his feelings to himself. Generally he could only recite symptoms: constant depression, inability to enjoy anything, inability to sleep, and constant anxiety, all of which were related to the memories of stalking and killing so many men. The worst flashback involved a senior Korean officer one hot summer afternoon. The moment of this kill in particular caused Matt constant nightmares and seemed to symbolize all the men he had terminated from ambush. He had told his story to several groups of medical students who had preceded the current clinical clerkship in psychiatry.

"I was hidden in the trees, maybe a hundred yards from where the North Koreans were filtering down the trail toward the south. I spotted this gook in my scope but couldn't get a good fix on him. The line of sight was poor, so I had to work my way down the hill always. I stalked the son of a bitch for fifteen, twenty minutes until they stopped to rest. This colonel went off to the side to take a leak, and that's how he was posed when I got him in the crosshairs . . . "

He paused, swallowing hard. I waited for him to continue.

" . . . I saw the bullet hit him right between the eyes. His whole fucking head exploded! I can't get it out of my head! I'm afraid to go to sleep at night because it all comes flooding back. Time after time. The nightmares are so real. There are times I can hardly stand it. He's just standing there and then suddenly his head is exploding; then there's just a big, bloody hole! God!"

He pounded his forehead, trying to hammer the images away. They were trapped in there, but he was their prisoner. He usually did not wish to talk about his other experiences, which would have been therapeutic for him. His condition was technically known as PTSD (post-traumatic stress disorder), which, unfortunately, is very difficult to treat, as it seems natural to want to avoid the memory of the pain instead of lovingly embracing the experience as a way of mastering it.

He also suffered from a "biological kindling" by his brain due to physical changes from the emotional trauma. The kindling also set off the "flashbacks," which in turn became his nightmares. I was treating him with only moderate success by prescribing a tricyclic anti-depressant to help him cope with his depression and, we hoped, lessen the "kindling" phenomenon in his brain. I had asked him to share with me and the medical students all of his traumas because I knew he could never recover without doing so.

I had been seeing Matt for about three years at intervals of every two months or so the morning he burst into my office. At the time, I had with me the five MSU medical students, one of whom was scheduled to interview him later that morning.

As he slammed the door, he blurted out, "Goddamn, cocksucking bastards! They cut my benefits way back! I won't have enough money to live on. They don't believe I've got PTSD. I laid my life on the line for this country, and now the bastards want me and my wife to starve! I'm going to kill them!"

"Who do you mean by 'them'?" I asked him.

"The fucking bureaucrats!" he screamed.

"I'm glad you can tell us how you feel," one of the students replied. "But are you serious about that?"

"You're damn right I'm serious. I've got the guns and I'm going down to the VA office in Grand Rapids and blow all their fucking heads off! I've still got my guns and I know how to use them."

The student looked anxiously over me.

"Steve," I interrupted the student, "will you take down all the details of Matt's problem? I need to go downstairs for just a few minutes. Matt may feel better as you chart the details of his pain."

The look on Steve's face asked me why I was abandoning him, but I knew Matt posed no threat to the students. The reason I was excusing myself was to find a VA security guard to come upstairs and keep Matt from leaving prematurely while I talked with one of the VA administrators there at the medical center. Michigan law requires that the intended victim must be warned of any physical threat if the physician deems it to be serious. The administrator called the VA regional office in Grand Rapids and Washington, where he received assurances that Matt's situation would be reviewed. We told officials in both locations of Matt's threat to kill someone because his benefits had been greatly reduced.

We also phoned the sheriff in Matt's hometown to ask him to keep an eye on Matt when he returned home. The bureaucrats in Washington promised a speedy review of his file to find out what had happened. I went back upstairs to tell Matt that the VA Administrative Services people were going to look into his situation, perhaps leading to resumption of all of his benefits.

"Promise you won't do anything until we hear from Washington," I said to him. "I need your assurance you won't hurt anyone or yourself in the meantime; otherwise, I'll have to hospitalize you against your will. I know you'll honor your word if you give it because we have logged a lot of hours together. I promise to see you every few days until this matter is resolved."

I saw he was extremely angry and depressed, but he finally agreed. He made eye contact with me as he made the promise.

I put my hand on his shoulder, and his eyes teared as he said,

"I respect and trust you, Doc. I won't do anything right now." With that he got up and left.

One of the students said, "Wow, that was scary!" and the others nodded in agreement.

The students and I monitored Matt's homicidal and suicidal risk factors every few days. About ten days later he arrived with a smile and tears in his eyes as he thanked us. His benefits had been restored in full. *I guess there's nothing like a little death threat to get people's attention and make them see the error of their ways,* I thought to myself.

"Did you feel I had betrayed your trust when I told Administration of your threat?" I asked him.

"Yes," he replied.

"I had to inform them, you see, because I knew you would do it. Besides, it's the law. I had no choice."

"I've always liked you, Dr. Turke," he said, with tears in his eyes as he turned to the med students sitting nearby. "He's not like the usual VA psychiatrist, you know." He turned back to me. "We've had some close moments, haven't we, Dr. Turke?"

"Yes, we have, Matt. Can I ask you a question?"

"Sure."

"You'll answer truthfully?"

"Yes."

"When you learned I had told Administration that you were going to kill those people in Grand Rapids, did you want to kill me then, too?"

"Yes, I felt like it. I'm sorry."

"Do you want to now?"

"No."

I smiled and said, "I'm glad. I didn't want to have to use my karate on you."

He laughed and left.

I looked at one of the medical students and said, "Still want to go into psychiatry?"

"Sure," she replied.

"I worry about your sanity," another student quipped.

A couple of years had passed since that episode and I hadn't seen Matt in some time when I received a letter from his wife saying that he had died of a massive heart attack. I felt sad for him, because at that time of his life he was just beginning to feel better about himself. Because he had liked me, he had repeated the story of his emotional anguish to each new group. Probably as many as sixty students had benefited from the telling of his story. It had been his "gift" to me for caring about him as a person, and in the process of the retelling he began to heal.

The Sniper was just one of approximately a hundred veterans I had seen and treated for PTSD. I liked and respected Matt and had empathy for his suffering. Sometimes the burden of seeing his misery had left me feeling dejected, but only for a short time, because I had trained myself to leave those feelings at the office as a means of self-preservation. Empathy is a desirable trait, but we must also be aware of countertransference. I recognized that I was sad in part because I had an inner loneliness of my own at the time. Perhaps the sadness I felt for Matt was also for myself.

On infrequent occasions I felt a certain tendency toward cynicism, which I worked hard at keeping out of my thoughts when giving psychiatric care at the hospital. I have a great respect for nearly all of the veterans I have treated, from World War II to the Persian Gulf. They deserve our caring and empathy and treatment resources, which are sparse and, at times, of poor quality. Unfortunately, there are many people in civilian life who harass these veterans and malign them without reason.

There were, however, too many men who had been wild and crazy or antisocial or alcoholics and substance abusers before they went to war, who in fact loved the war. Then they came home after having fried their brains some more with alcohol and other drugs. They returned, asked for disability, and let their "surrogate mothers" (wives) take care of them as they just sat in front of the TV drinking beer, wasting their lives away.

The Sniper had not been one of those, but his life had been wasted anyway.

Chapter 2

It's a common perception that psychiatrists often enter the profession in an attempt to solve their own psychological problems. There may be some accuracy in that assessment, although such conclusions can often be too simplistic. I find it somewhat true in my own case, however. Looking back on my life, I find that my progress from a shy, overprotected child born to German emigrant parents to what I have become by my sixty-third year was significantly aided by the choice in my career.

I don't recall any sudden flash of insight when I decided to become a psychiatrist. The choice evolved instead from my need to respect myself rather than to please my parents. The need was a conscious feeling that came after I first considered becoming a medical missionary to get and keep the love of my father. This was also influenced by my desire to gain the affections of a girl I admired in college.

My decision to become a psychiatrist focused for me in my junior year in medical school at the University of Iowa during my clerkship in psychiatry. My role model was Paul Huston, Ph.D., M.D., the chairman of the Department of Psychiatry, who had arranged for a summer externship in psychiatry for me along with a research stipend before taking the clerkship. (My research project compared the personalities of breast cancer patients with those having cervical cancer. Breast cancer patients appeared to have low anxiety, were overcontrolled, and tended to have a religious value system. Cervical cancer patients appeared to have overt anxiety and were more promiscuous.) Dr. Paul often had the students over to his home for Pepsi, pizza, and conversation. Over the years there he became a surrogate father for me. I now also have students over to my condo for Pepsi, pizza, and conversation.

My memories of childhood are fairly extensive. I am grateful that I can recall the joy and pain of those formative years, which were often characterized by a great many fears and anxieties. Low self-esteem, shyness, dependency, an inability to share feelings, and inner loneliness marked those years and continue, to some degree, to this day.

My parents came from Remscheid, Germany, joining the flood of immigrants passing through Ellis Island, New York, in 1929. When they arrived in New York City, the family name was Tüerke, which, I've been told, dates back to the first German crusade (1147), in which my ancestor was the sole survivor. Legend has it that when he returned to Germany he was referred to as "the Turk." Archives in Berlin authenticate the story, and our family crest has Saracen towers and bows and arrows on it. An immigration judge, in all his wisdom, Americanized our name to Turke. My mother and father had been married aboard ship by the captain, apparently conceiving me on the high seas, since I was born nine months later, on June 23, 1930, in a New York City charity hospital, delivered by an intern. It was the Great Depression and a bad time to be an immigrant. We began life in America as guests of my father's sister and her husband. We were soon joined by his brother.

I was the firstborn and was doted on by everyone, especially my uncles, often getting more affection from them than from my father, who rarely spent time with me. I was always afraid of my father, even up to my years in college. Initially, my fear was physical, but it changed in my midteens to dread over his displeasure. My parents had been childhood sweethearts. Romance turned to reality, though, after they married. My father made all the decisions, in typical German tradition, while Mother got hypertension and headaches.

My aunts and uncles loved me and would praise me for the smallest things. I had my own pot for defecation and would often perform to their applause. I would bring it into the dining room while everyone was eating and proceed to use it with great gusto while they all applauded my accomplishment. Heady stuff for a two-year-old. It began to wear a little thin by the time I reached four. I ended this family tradition when I had my own children.

When I was about four we left my aunt and uncle's apartment and moved in with an elderly woman who owned a large house.

She waived the rent in exchange for my mother working in her home and taking care of her. Father got a job as a stock clerk at Oxford University Press, near Union Square in Manhattan. Often emotionally remote for us, he now became physically distant, working long hours between subway commutes from Brooklyn that took over an hour each way. I saw him only on Saturday nights and Sundays, but even then he didn't spend time with me outside of going to church.

As a young child I spent my days playing in the dirt outside the house, constantly watched by Mother, who warned me about blacks, Jews, Italians, and "strangers." I was not allowed to go beyond the area of the house and had no friends. I was fearful, bashful, shy, eager to please, nonassertive, and painfully well behaved. It's interesting to note that as I grew up many of my best friends were Jewish, Hispanic, Italian, or Afro-American.

I once strayed a half block from home and returned with a spring flower I had picked for my mother. She shamed and scolded me and made me take it back to where I had picked it. I stuck it back in the ground but held out little hope for its survival. I never brought my mother anything again.

At the age of five I ran down the block to watch some children playing punchball. I watched from behind a tree because I felt so inferior. I felt they would laugh at me because of the clothes I wore and my shyness. I went back home without speaking a word, which in my case would have been mostly German and some broken English with a Brooklyn accent, a very humiliating and shameful combination in my own mind.

I was extremely afraid of spiders as a child but somehow drawn to them. I became a spider hunter and caught them in dark places, imprisoning them in glass jars with airholes in the lids. I tossed twigs into the jars and watched the spiders spin the webs used to ensnare the ants and flies I threw in for food. Some twenty-five years later I learned that in the subconscious the spider may represent the destructive mother, who also ensnares her young in her web and sometimes eats (destroys) them. Mother hated the spiders Strangely, my father enjoyed feeding the spiders, too. It was my first feeling of power; I was catching and controlling something that I feared.

We walked to church every Sunday as a family. Because we were so poor, we never had a car until I left home for college years later. We walked in every type of weather, despite the fact that the church was over forty minutes from home. I hated it, especially since the minister's wife often had me say the prayer in Sunday school. I would worry about it all the previous week and was terrified to the extent that I could not remember three sentences.

I had few friends because of my parents' disapproval and didn't know how to talk to anyone except my parents, with whom I shared nothing personal. The old lady we lived with died, and we had to move. I saw her dead in her casket and didn't understand what that meant. Mother said she was in heaven. I couldn't comprehend the concept because the old woman was still lying there.

I was six when we moved into our own place, a run-down duplex just down the street from the old lady's house. At the end of the block was a fence and a railroad track, with a power rail separating us from a tough Italian section. My father's mother arrived from Germany and moved in with my aunt. It was nearly two miles away, but we used it as our address so I could get into the PS 97 school district and not have to go to the Italian neighborhood public school.

I often walked the two miles to my aunt's for lunch. Oma (Grandmother) fed me potato pancakes with butter and jam and treated me with affection, while acting like a Marine Corps drill sergeant to her own adult children. She was only four feet, ten inches tall, and I called her "Kleine Ameise", "little ant."

School beckoned for me, and I was terrified of it and my own inadequacies. I didn't know how to talk to other kids and was a classic underachiever who couldn't even take off or put on his own galoshes. I feared and resented the teachers and was always afraid of being called on. Over the next four years I was often "sick" in order to avoid school and being laughed at, particularly when we studied Turkey or the Turks. I felt everyone would make fun of me because of my name. It was at this time I began to learn English and developed a Brooklyn accent rather than a German one. I was very ashamed of my parents because they still spoke like "foreigners." I was proud to be an American!

When I was seven, my sister, Frieda, was born. She was named after my mother. I had been named after Father and hated it. I resented my sister because she got all the attention from my father, notice I never received from him despite Mother begging him to give it to me. As a result Mother became even more possessive of me, which I feared and enjoyed at the same time.

In the new neighborhood I finally made some close friends, whose names sounded like a convention of the United Nations. There were Germans, Russians, English, and Jews, along with Tom "the Retard" and Dick "the Bully," whom I feared. Tom was five years older than the rest of us and had girlie magazines, which he read on the front stoop of his apartment building. Mother told me if I looked at them I'd go blind and then to hell later on. Since I now wear glasses the assumption is that I might have glanced briefly at some of the pictures. As to the hell part, we'll have to wait and see.

We played punchball and stoopball, and, at age eight, I began playing baseball in the sandlot in the Italian area adjacent to the railroad track. We'd all climb the fence and cross the railroad track, being careful not to get "fried" on the power rail. I was a very good baseball player, and as a result my self-esteem improved. I even had some new father figures and role models, the Brooklyn Dodgers, especially Don Newcombe, Roy Campanella, and Jackie Robinson.

For some reason I began having recurring nightmares in which I'd find my mother's body encased in the cement blocks that separated the public sidewalk from the entrance of the houses on our block. After one of these dreams, I got in bed with my parents and cuddled up to mother, noticing her breasts as I did. Father got extremely angry and told me to get back to my room immediately. I then had dreams of the Frankenstein monster!

In the summer of 1938, my mother, sister, and grandmother and I left New York to visit my mother's family in Remscheid, traveling on the USS *Hamburg*. I was dressed in a sailor suit. My favorite uncle had given me boxing gloves so I could learn to be more assertive. I loudly proclaimed that I was Joe Louis and was going to knock out my cousin of the same age in Germany, who would be Max Schmeling.

Our quarters on board were at the very bottom of the ship, but we did have a porthole, because I can remember seeing London at six o'clock one morning. There were children's parties on board ship, but no one ever talked to me. I was alone as usual. When presents were given out by the crew at the parties, I always got the worst ones, compared to the other kids, whose parents were wealthier.

When we arrived in Germany, I was very ill at ease with my mother's family except for two uncles who doted on me. Ironically, they were SS officers who would talk to strangers in black raincoats who visited frequently and walked away from the rest of us.

My Joe Louis imitation was short-lived—one punch, as I recall. My cousin, Hans Walter, bloodied my nose and shamed me in front of all the family who had turned out to watch the spectacle.

My uncle Otto took me to the Hitler Youth camps, where children were being trained to be soldiers. I remember being treated well, and the boys appeared interested in meeting an American from New York. I got my first erection while in one of the camps. It wasn't a love affair with Nazism but rather the metal pole I was rubbing against as I climbed. The erection felt so good I didn't want to come down. I had no idea what it meant, since talk of sex had always been taboo in our house. I thought I had discovered something unique and exciting.

Uncle Otto secretly taught me German swearwords by giving me a mark (dollar) whenever I learned to say one correctly. My mother was shocked by this behavior, which made it all the more pleasurable for me. Uncle Otto got me a Hitler haircut, taught me to "Sieg Heil," and took me to large stadiums to hear Nazi speakers exhorting the masses. On one occasion I got to hear Hitler himself, whom I was taught to admire for unifying the German people. My uncle accepted me, taught me manly things, and immunized me somewhat from the pious, subservient religiosity of my parents.

Both my uncles were killed in the war. I especially mourned

Uncle Otto. I had loved walking with him through the Black Forest and seeing old castles, particularly the ruin called Dragon's Mount overlooking the Rhine. Hitler invaded Poland shortly after we left for New York. I have always wondered what would have happened to my life if he had done so sooner.

Thirty years later I was watching TV and saw a man walking suspiciously around my condo at Bay Valley Resort in Bay City, Michigan. He appeared to be my age. The doorbell rang and he introduced himself to me as Hans Walter, my cousin. He had sold his toy business and was now touring the United States with his girlfriend, having been divorced some years ago. With a straight face, I walked him into the lower level of my condo, where I have a Japanese *dojo* to practice my Shotokan karate. I looked at him menacingly and made some aggressive moves in his direction, saying he was now going to be punished for bloodying my nose back in Germany. He looked very frightened until I joked with him and had a hearty laugh.

It is a shocking experience to see someone look so old for his age. Hans was now rather portly and gray. I almost hurt myself carrying his suitcase upstairs, which, he informed me as we got to the top, was filled with German beer.

The year after we got back from Germany I got to go to the 1939 World's Fair. I have memories of watching Charlie McCarthy and Edgar Bergen at the Chase and Sanborn exhibit and of standing in line for Heinz baked beans and of watching lightning being made at the Westinghouse exhibit and riding in small GM gas cars. I nearly met a premature end while riding the Ferris wheel when I nearly fell out leaning out to peek over the wall of the outdoor "girlie show."

It's interesting how instinctive the sexual urges are. In addition to my Ferris wheel misadventure, I continued to succumb to the allure of the female body without having the slightest idea why.

I was a very shy, clumsy stage performer and was laughed at for my acting attempts as a frog in the eighth grade "chorus line," although I used the rehearsal sessions to further my knowledge of the female anatomy. Four of the class's most attractive girls had to practice curtsying and in so doing crossed their legs, thus enabling my friends and me to look up their dresses. Interesting but not quite as good as climbing an exercise pole.

At recess the "Farmer in the Dell" game was played by the whole class. The most popular male was always the farmer, who then chose a "wife"—the most popular girl, of course. I was never chosen farmer or for any of the better roles. Not even the "rat." I was usually the cheese, and I can recall the everyone clapping and singing, "The cheese stands alone." And so I was.

My lack of social graces slowly went away as I got more and more into sports at PS 97. I became renowned for playing "the wall" in punchball. As my self-image improved so did my desire to rid myself of my fear of the school bullies who had plagued me over the years. One by one I sought them out and methodically began to beat them up to get even for all the physical abuse and shame I had suffered at their hands.

On one occasion in front of a crowd of kids I had one bully on the ground, punching him in the face, when I heard my father's whistle to come home. The whistle meant to run there immediately. When I didn't respond Father came and got me, pulling me off my opponent in front of everyone and humiliating me. The bully didn't laugh, though. And neither did anyone else.

My last fight turned out to be anticlimactic. I challenged the number-one bully of PS 97 to an afternoon fistfight. He had been one of my biggest tormentors for years. The entire class turned out. Trouble is, we were both afraid of each other. We made menacing motions toward each other like a couple of banty roosters on tranquillizers for nearly ten minutes without any blows being struck. Then we both walked away, I called it a moral victory. He never bothered me again.

My relationship with my father continued to depress me. One time my dog, Queenie, urinated on the carpet, then snapped at my father when he struck her. He grabbed her by the neck and threw her down the cellar stairs. I made a motion to hit Father, and he threw me down the stairs, too, then beat me with a plastic belt until I bled. Mother tried to intervene and he hit her with the belt, too. I wondered how such a religious man could be so cruel. I hated him.

Even more so when, several months later, I was given a pet

rooster by someone Father knew at church. I named him Lollipop, which aptly demonstrated my emotional immaturity at that age. Trouble was Lollipop had a habit of going "Cock-a-doodle-doo!" every morning and the neighbors complained to Father about being wakened. Father did everything for the neighbors and was idealized by them, but he never did anything for Mother.

One Sunday noon shortly after the complaints started, we were served a "chicken" dinner by Father. After we had finished dessert, Father asked us how Lollipop had tasted. My hatred for my father grew even more intense as I bolted from the dining room to throw up my meal.

Mother tied me to her apron strings but never taught me how to brush or floss my teeth or wash my hair or cut my nails. She did everything for me, including bathing me until I was in my teens. I asked her once about the "sticky fluid" in my pajamas in the morning. She said not to worry about it. I was the "king" but also a "baby" emotionally. In many ways, though, I was fearless, and I would walk alone in bad neighborhoods and take long bike rides in heavy traffic. I backed down from no one.

I had to get glasses, which I seldom wore out of deference to my already low self-esteem. Add the four-eyed look to my crooked teeth, which we couldn't afford to have fixed, and what you had was your basic self-proclaimed social outcast. I also had to wear the same clothes to school every day, which Mother washed dutifully every night.

My father, the religious zealot, would occasionally do the parental thing by taking me to Coney Island. He did have an ulterior motive, however. The best ride in Steeplechase Park involved racing against five other mechanical horses that went around the park's perimeter. The only exit was in front of a large audience where a hundred men might spend their entire afternoon. The stage and exit were filled with hidden air jets. Three clowns with electric "prods" would get the women to walk over the air jets with their hands up and blow their dresses over their heads. The audience would cheer and throw coins to the clowns. Father would whistle his approval. We'd stay there for hours. I pretended to be embarrassed but secretly enjoyed it.

Church brought on other social traumas for me. As I mentioned earlier, I was called on to pray frequently in Sunday school. I would attempt to memorize a prayer prior to going, but I always forgot it when the minister's wife called on me. She did it for years and I hated her for it, little knowing that the activity would help me build confidence for public speaking in later years.

We had a church revival meeting for which a renowned evangelist was invited to speak. He was also the editor in chief for our church's paper in the United States. I became his "gofer" and assistant all week. He liked me and on the last night of the revival he took me into the church basement to "thank me" for being so helpful. He tried to kiss me several times. I ran away and told my father, who, of course, punished me for "lying!"

When I was thirteen, my father's religiosity took on an added dimension when he went through another religious conversion experience. As the fervency of his praying grew so did my discomfort with him. Now he began putting his hands on the inside of my thigh during sermons and he frequently cried. No more cigars, *Police Gazette*, or steeplechase at Coney Island. The minister let him lead prayer meetings on Wednesday nights, which I was forced to attend. My embarrassment grew intensely when he cried during his own sermons. His closeness to God brought him no nearer to me. My mother yelled at him often for not spending any time with me or her.

I was just entering puberty but didn't have a clue about sex between men and women. My mother was grossly protective of me. Even at this age she continued to bathe me and wash my hair in the bathtub.

My first date, to a movie after school, was with Gladys Walker, whom I had adored from a distance. We held hands and touched cheeks, and I was in ecstasy. Socially I made another quantum leap during a confrontation with another school bully. When I laughed at him over some incident, he charged me. The schoolbook I slammed in his face slowed him down, broke his nose, and bloodied his face. He began to cry as he stood there dripping blood. I felt no remorse, however. He always avoided me from then on and my reputation for toughness continued to grow!

My graduation from PS 97 was marked not by the joy of accomplishment, but by the fear of the unknown, coupled with the negative relationship I had with my parents. My father was working as usual, and I told Mother not to attend graduation, since I was ashamed of her, too. I walked home alone with my diploma and pin. I feared going to Franklin K. Lane High School, a Brooklyn high school known for its toughs who carried weapons. My parents told me there would be no dancing, smoking, card playing, or pool playing, or going out with girls. My remaining options were to become a very good athlete and to stay in my room alone listening to the Brooklyn Dodgers on the radio.

I started high school at Franklin Knight Lane, where the students were mostly Italian, Jewish, and black. School was hard, since I had never developed any study habits. I made the baseball team my freshman year. I had a good fastball, sweeping curve, and change of pace. My fellow pitcher Bob Grimm became Rookie of the Year for the New York Yankees some years later. I had a lightning move to first base, surpassed in quickness only by the move I made the day I caught my penis in the zipper of my baseball uniform.

I had immediate status as an athlete. My gym teachers were always matching me with the toughest blacks in boxing class. I was still shy, though, and didn't know how to socialize or dance and avoided all school social activities. I didn't know how to talk to people except about sports and movies. Despite my social shortcomings, I was well liked by the intellectuals as well as by the jocks.

Gangs from South Brooklyn and East New York would periodically attack our baseball team in front of the school during practice. They used knives and chains, and we defended ourselves with baseball bats. The next day the school toughs would come with guns to protect us in the event the gangs came back. In school there were no overt racial issues to speak of. Strangely enough, I related well academically and athletically to all the students, no matter what their race or creed, and the toughs respected me as a person.

Baseball was my life during that time. I played on a team comprised of star players from other high school teams in the summer and played in a high school league during the school year. Our team frequently went to Ebbets Field early in the morning to get the best seats in the left field bleachers and catch balls during batting practice. Then we'd be off to Coney Island for Nathan's hot dogs and french fries and then to walk the famous boardwalk before going home.

When we went to Brighton Beach, the rest of the team would bring their girlfriends while I was always alone. My job was to cover the couples completely with blankets so they could "neck," then stand watch for cops and toughs. I still longed for Gladys Walker, who was dating a senior with whom I felt I couldn't compete. I also had a crush on a Jewish girl, Sondra Fisher, but was afraid to ask her out; I think she knew because she signed my graduation book with: "Love." To this day I regret not having asked her out. All my life, my most intimate friends have been Jewish. I often wonder if part of the reason had something to do with my "Nazi" heritage.

At sixteen I was asked to pitch for a baseball team in a summer league in Bellerose, Long Island. The team was composed of the best players from the high school teams that played each other during the school year. To get to Bellerose I had to walk to the elevated subway line to get to Jamaica and then catch a bus to Bellerose. The trip took one-and-a-half to two hours.

I met Dolly at one of the baseball games, and we liked each other a great deal. We would walk in the rain and talk a lot. She introduced me to her parents, whom I liked and respected. Dolly was beautiful, intelligent, and Catholic. When I kissed her, she told me that I was "special," because otherwise she would not have allowed it.

I knew Father would not be happy with my dating outside our religion, so I never mentioned Dolly to him. When the baseball season ended, I continued to want to go to Bellerose. I told my parents the truth about wanting to see Dolly. They forbade me to ever see her again and said that they would not let me go to Bellerose again. I was shattered. I didn't know how to tell her and shamefully dropped out of her life without a word.

I saw her again a year later. She was holding hands with the third baseman on our team. She didn't look at me and never talked to me again. I hated Father for his intolerance and I hated myself because I could not express my feelings.

Gladys Walker wrote in my book, "As long as pussy has a tail my love for you will never fail." Although it didn't occur to me at the time, I now like to believe that Gladys wasn't talking about her cat.

In addition to baseball, the movies were everything to me, particularly the adventure movies: *Gunga Din, Beau Geste, Lives of a Bengal Lancer, and Drums along the Mohawk,* all of which are in my video library now. Movies were my refuge from my parents. I hated when the movies ended. Coming out into the bright sunlight and hearing the traffic and noise was a crushing return to reality. The World War II movies made me try to join the marines, but I was too young.

Woody Allen, who attended PS 100 in Brooklyn about the same time, also talks about the movies being a refuge from his family. He was also a good athlete.

I was an ardent fan of the Big Bands: Duke Ellington, Tommy and Jimmy Dorsey, Count Basie, Artie Shaw, and, of course, Harry James. I met Harry in the midseventies when I went backstage the night he played at the Interlochen Center for the Arts in northern Michigan.

I said, "Hello, Harry. I had your picture on my wall all through high school."

Without batting an eye he said, "I thought you looked familiar!"

I got a job working at Oxford University Press with my father. I played stickball in the street during lunch hour with the other male employees. I could drive a ball far and was known as a "three-sewer man." It was exciting to play ball, dodging traffic and sometimes climbing a fire escape to retrieve the ball from the top of a building.

Everyone in my school and church was wearing pegged pants, like the "zoot suiters." My parents opposed this vigorously but ultimately allowed me to have a slight "peg" in my pants. A ninety-year-old man had died next door, and my father bought me one of his dark blue jackets to wear with my gray pants. I was invited to a friend's house where everyone danced the "Lindy Hop" to records. I was attracted to a very pretty girl at one of these parties. She laughed at me for wearing an old-fashioned jacket with a belt in the back, but I didn't know why until a friend told me later. I will never forget it. I left the party right after she did that.

My parents attended only one baseball game of all those I played in. I pitched a no-hit, no-run game and hit two balls off the left field screen for doubles to win the game. The umpire, a former National League umpire, made a speech about me at the end of the game to the people in the stands. My mother applauded. I think Father was moved, but he said very little. We walked all the way home, since my parents still couldn't afford a car. Not a word was spoken during the walk.

I made the All City team and was voted best athlete of my high school class. The honor should have gone to my copitcher Leonard Jaffe, who was later signed by the Yankees. The girls in Honors English got all the intellectuals to vote for me, outvoting the jocks, who wanted Lenny. I had an offer from the Pittsburgh Pirates to go play triple-A ball. I doubted I could make it in the big leagues and did not want to be a "baseball bum."

I attended graduation from high school alone. Father was working as always, and I was still ashamed to go with Mother. I never went places with my friends because I had to be home early, before 11:00 P.M. The gang would come by my house and chant, "Womanless one, come out, come out!" I occasionally heard them chanting in my dreams. Sometimes even now when I'm lonely I picture the scene.

One member of our gang was over seven feet tall. His feet were huge, as was, of course, all the rest of him. When he did the Lindy Hop, the floor would move. When we played basketball against him on the playground, he'd get all the rebounds and dunks until we worked on a way to control him: elbowing him in the ribs and then pulling down his shorts as he went up to dunk.

I completed high school having kissed about five girls, all at church camps in the summer. I never even fondled a girl! Although I have regrets about this, I always believed in romantic love and some of the values my parents taught me I now hold dear. Unfortunately (or fortunately), some of my missed erotic experiences in adolescence were acted out during my midlife crisis.

My fantasies, baseball and the movies, plus the value system

I learned at church, kept me going during my adolescence. I was a romantic, saving myself for my one true love, who was a composite of all the best traits of all the girls I knew and the movie queens I had watched on the big screen. I didn't even know about masturbation. I had to wait until after I was married to discover that skill.

My father and I developed some togetherness of a sort in that we both liked monster movies. He took me to see *Frankenstein, Dracula, The Wolf Man* and *The Mummy.* We never talked on the way to or from the theaters. I had nightmares about monsters through the years until I was sixteen. I didn't realize at the time that the nightmares represented my fear of my father. My hatred of him gave additional unconscious pleasure when the monsters were destroyed at the end of the film, perhaps leading to unconscious guilt as well.

When I graduated from high school I was still somewhat of a social misfit, with numerous personality flaws. I remained very dependent on my parents, isolated socially, a child unable to express his feelings. I knew nothing about dressing and grooming and was naive about sexuality and life in general. I was also moralistic and judgmental. On the outside I appeared to be the all-American boy, the star athlete, clean-cut, strong, silent, but inside I was a frightened child seeking approval and fearing rejection and afraid of the world. My reaction formation to these deficits was to be arrogant, fearless, and independent.

Chapter 3

My journey toward psychiatry began without my awareness in the summer of 1948 when I left Brooklyn for a small church college in Le Mars, Iowa, approximately fifty miles south of Sioux City. I was led to this far-flung outpost of civilization by contacts our minister in Brooklyn had established.

My high school yearbook listed where everyone was going to college: Columbia, New York University, Dartmouth, etc. My school was Western Union. Everyone thought I was going to be a telegrapher! Western Union was a church college and a union of the Evangelical and United Brethren (EUB) church. The name was changed to Westmar College shortly after my arrival, but obviously not in time for my high school yearbook.

The very fact that I was going to college at all was a bit of a miracle, considering the economic status of my parents. Arrangements had been made for me to work and borrow my way through school. I was hired to paint the dormitories, garden and weed, and do odd jobs in the maintenance department. I also went out for the football team. I would get up at 2:00 A.M. and paint the dorms until 8:00 A.M. and then practice football.

The school was accredited and had a large enrollment of pretheology students. There was, of course, a great deal of hostility between the "God squad" members and the "jocks."

Most of the students were from the Midwest, but there were perhaps twelve people in the 1,000 Mile Club, which consisted of students attending from greater distances. I was the only New Yorker and wore my Brooklyn AC jacket constantly to retain my identity. I was envious of the lettermen who were BMOCs. My high school in Brooklyn abandoned football after a player was killed, so I had no previous experience playing this sport. The team was coached by Dick Crayne, an All-American from the University of Iowa. I played right halfback in a single wing offense. My assignment was to knock down the tackle or the end so the other backs could go through the hole. Most of the time I rode the pine. We played all the games at night with poor light and my night vision without glasses was poor and it was very hard for me to see the ball. "Braille ball," I called it.

I once had a tooth knocked out at the University of South Dakota, who beat us "big." Some thirty-six years later, when I was on the Department of Psychiatry faculty at USD, I returned to the football field to look for my tooth. No luck.

College was the first time I had ever been away from my family for any length of time. I had very little money and few clothes and didn't know how to brush my teeth, floss, wash my hair, sew, or do laundry. I was happy to be away from my parents, though. The freedom was exhilarating. I continued to be "good," no drinking or smoking and dates to church with kissing being the only physical contact with girls. I didn't stay out late and didn't use street language. Perhaps I had seen too many John Wayne movies.

My fears were dealt with by pretending to be a "tough guy" from Brooklyn. I refused to wear my freshman beanie and did not get off the sidewalk for sophomores as was expected. In fact, I pushed them off the sidewalk! Big mistake. First my dormitory room was hosed down with water. Later that evening while I was walking downtown, three carloads of sophomores caught me and loaded me in the trunk of one of the cars. I was taken to the basement of one of the dormitories, stripped, and held down while large black spiders were placed on my body. My pubic hair was then shaved off and my privates painted with tincture of merthioate, followed by analgesic balm heat compound. By then it was well past dark and I was taken ten to fifteen miles out in the Iowa countryside and dumped off after being allowed to dress in T-shirt, slacks, and shoes with no socks.

Every time I found a farmhouse to get help, the dogs would come after me. I eventually found the highway and hitched back to Le Mars, getting there about 6:00 A.M.

In my second year I met Laverne Partridge, a student from Montana who was very religious. She was also very beautiful, and I was smitten with her. After several dates, she told me not to get "serious" and I learned that she was having a date with a handsome pretheology student in our dormitory. I was extremely jealous. I knew the curfew at the women's dorm was 11:00 P.M., so I pulled a chair in front of the men's dorm and waited for the guy to come home from his date. I was not certain what my intentions were, but I knew I wanted to ask him questions. He never returned that night. I waited until 3:00 A.M. I was devastated and did not date for a very long time after that.

There was a religious revival week scheduled at the EUB church that I attended, and I made a pledge to become a medical missionary to Nigeria, where the church had a mission. I thought Laverne would come back to me if I did . . . and perhaps my father would love me. I also wanted to help those in need, perhaps because of my childhood deprivation and perhaps to reduce guilt about my inner anger.

I played baseball, pitching and playing center field for the college. My study habits were poor, but I managed a B average. I got my letter sweater in the second year and wore it proudly all the time. I was now accepted by the "jocks" and the "pretheos," and my identity as a religious premed athlete gave me status on campus, kind of a man for all reasons.

I continued to date superficially, movies and church dates, but no touching other than kissing. My sensual repression continued. I still didn't even know what masturbation was! I dated a girl for a time, who got quite serious about me in my junior year.

I decided to transfer to the University of Iowa in Iowa City for my fourth year. My credits transferred readily and I thought this would enhance my chances for admission to a medical school. My grade-point average of 3.2 would not get me into most medical schools. The University of Iowa took some nonresidents, but I thought my chances for acceptance into its medical school were only fair, except for my wishes to be a medical missionary.

During my year at Iowa as a senior I took mostly psychology courses, organic chemistry, and English literature.

My minister at Le Mars contacted the EUB church in Iowa City, and housing was found for me near the central campus. I was to live with and take care of an elderly widower, sharing his bedroom. This proved to be a difficult time for me. The mattress he bought for me at an auction was infested with lice, and his authoritarian attitude reminded me of my father. I attended the EUB church, which was about twenty miles out in the country in an Amish community. I still didn't have a car, nor did I know how to drive. I had to walk everywhere.

I wrote a letter to the editor of the campus newspaper liberally quoting Saint Paul about the lasciviousness and loose morals on campus. Even today I still feel shame when I recall the letter. Naive pomposity is not a very compelling trait.

Two nurses who were single and rather unattractive regularly drove me to church on Sundays in the country. I was very much of a loner, did no dating, and studied hard to get A's in my course so I might get into medical school. I learned that I was fourteenth on the alternate list for the freshman class, which had 116 students.

A former girlfriend from Westmar wrote to me and told me she was coming to Iowa City for a teachers' conference. The two nurses at the church put her up for two nights in their apartment. One afternoon while my landlord was away with his grown children, she came over and we lay down on the bed and started kissing. I touched only her face and hands. I lay on top of her, fully clothed, and soon she started moaning and writhing about. I became frightened, felt she was ill and wanted to call an ambulance. She told me she was OK. We never saw each other again. Some years later I learned something new, realizing she had had an orgasm! Naive stupidity doesn't work really well either.

My landlord died of a heart attack while going to the bathroom, his final movement being of fatal dimensions. Naked he came into the world; nearly naked he departed. Not a pretty sight. I was allowed to stay there for several weeks longer until summer break occurred.

I received my B.A. at commencement on June 6, 1952, alone again, as I had been at my two previous graduations. I returned to Brooklyn to wait for a letter from the dean of the medical school. Instead I got a notice from the draft board to report for a preinduction physical. Fortunately, I received a letter from Iowa at the same time indicating that I had been accepted to the medical school. I was overjoyed and my parents were very proud.

The summer after receiving my B.A. degree from Iowa, I spent some time visiting my aunt and uncle in West Hartford, Connecticut. My uncle was an engineer at Royal Typewriter Company and rather well-to-do. Summers in Connecticut were pleasant. My uncle and aunt doted on me, as they had no children of their own, and I enjoyed riding in their new cars, taking trips with them, and staying in their nice home. They also allowed me "freedom," a wasted benefit, since I continued to be well-behaved.

One of my uncle's subordinates had a daughter who was starting nurses' training at Flower Fifth Avenue Hospital in New York City. She happened to be visiting her parents in Hartford at the same time I was there. We all went to the beach together, where Rosemarie Lengsfeld and I met. I was immediately very attracted to her, since she was very pretty, my own age, rather shy, and reserved like me.

Rosemarie had been born in New York, but then her parents returned to Germany, settling in Silesia near the Polish border. She and her mother and sister escaped from Russian Mongolian troops who raped others while she hid in the closet. She also survived the Dresden incendiary bombing by Allied forces. Her father was captured by the Russians and became psychotic. Rosemarie was able to return to the United States because of her citizenship. She worked as a maid for a wealthy Stamford, Connecticut, family to earn money to bring her parents back to the United States. Her father returned with her mother and sister, and they then moved to Hartford. Her father remained somewhat strange and had unusual religious beliefs and dietary habits. He would not eat meat, so he purchased vegetables and fixed them to look like meat. He joined the Rosicrucians and adopted unusual religious tenets, which were secret but dominated the family.

Rosemarie and I dated a good deal that summer and had many things in common. However, I was affection-starved and she was rather reserved by nature. On one occasion I remember taking her across the street from the nurses' quarters into Central Park so we could spoon. We kissed once in the bushes, but then we realized what a dangerous place we were in after dark. We hurried back to her dorm and never did that again.

We wrote to each other when I went back to Iowa City. That

Christmas I returned to New York where I proposed to Rosemarie because I did not wish to lose her to someone else. Also, I had started losing my hair the previous year and was feeling desperate, feeling that no one would want me. She agreed to transfer to Iowa the following fall. I gave her an engagement ring with a diamond so small that one would need a magnifying glass to see it. I returned to the second half of my first year in the medical school.

The first semester had been a disaster for me. The first day in school we were told to look at the person sitting to the left and the person to the right and that one of the three would not be there at the end of the year. Although my IQ was 126, I assumed that everyone was much brighter than me (probably true) and that I was the most stupid person ever enrolled at Iowa. I spent all my free hours studying, usually until two o'clock every morning. I found it hard to concentrate in class, felt extremely anxious, overate (ice cream—frozen mother's milk), and had strong sensual urges unrelieved by "wet dreams." I allowed myself a few hours off every Saturday night, going to the Student Union (with my books) alone to watch *The Colgate Comedy Hour* at 7:00 P.M., followed by the Sid Caesar *Show of Shows* and *Your Hit Parade.*

At the end of the first year I got D's in all my courses except a C in physiology. I felt so anxious and depressed that I had severe pains in the lower colon, which the Student Health Services said were "stress." I was told, along with five other students, that I would have to take a comprehensive examination on all of the first year subject matter before I could start the second year. Failure meant being dropped from school. The associate dean of students suggested I consider pharmacy college, but I applied to Clinical Psychology at Iowa and at William and Mary in Virginia, just in case. I was rejected by Iowa in psychology because of not enough courses in statistics but was accepted at William and Mary.

I was invited to Dayton, Ohio, by the Department of World Missions of the EUB church. They told me if I still wanted to be a medical missionary, they would pay for part of my medical student tuition for the next three years. They would assign me to Sierra Leone or Nigeria. I accepted and the financial stress lessened somewhat. I was able to study better for my comprehensive examination with Rosemarie by my side most of the summer. We planned our wedding and had $270 to spend for it. We had enough money left for subway fare to Grand Central Station in NYC and train fare to Iowa City.

Our wedding took place in the Church of Peace in Brooklyn, New York. I had daydreams of running away, felt I had made a big mistake, but recognized that it was probably part of the "jitters." Rosemarie looked very pretty but was as anxious as I was. I had fantasies the entire month before about how, after the wedding, we would change and I would get to see her body for the first time. After an alcohol-free reception, where potato salad, coleslaw, and cold cuts were served, Rosemarie told me that her sister would help her change and I would have to use another room! My romantic fantasy was shattered because my protest about this was completely ignored.

My best man, from Iowa City, drove Rosemarie and me to the subway station to get to Grand Central; we were met at the entrance by my parents. My father wished me well, smiling with a tear in his eye. He shook my hand, and I touched him on the shoulder. Mother was crying. She threw her arms around me and erotically forced her tongue into the back of my mouth. I thought I would throw up! My mind was flooded with images of Mother bathing me, keeping me away from other women. I told Rosemarie and a few close friends about that, but not until more than ten years later.

We had all our things in two suitcases and a football duffel bag. The train ride to Iowa City took two days, and we slept one night in the coach chairs.

My minister from Iowa City allowed us to use his cabin at the church camp for three days before my comprehensive exam was to take place. On arrival Rosemarie showered and undressed by herself with the door locked. I did the same. We got into bed in our pajamas, and suddenly there was a tremendous racket outside. The minister had brought about twelve church members with him to give us a "shivaree." I had no sense of humor about this; my erect penis went totally limp, and the longer the group stayed, the angrier I got. The street kid in me wanted to start a serious fight after four hours of unwanted company. They left just in time, but the evening had been a disaster and would continue as such. Rosemarie and I knew exactly nothing about sex, and it showed in our interactions with each other. What I had learned about sex in school was a psychiatrist telling me, "Sex is the most fun you can have without laughing!" Up to this point I hadn't even broken into a grin.

I recall an incident of which I was most proud while taking social psychology in my senior year of undergraduate school. There were pantie raids taking place on campus where groups of male students would break into the women's dorms and forcibly steal any panties they could find. The professor asked in class how this situation could be dealt with. I suggested women students donate panties and we would place these in a large bin in front of Old Capital in the center of campus and let anyone take them who wanted them. The rest of the class felt this was a great idea, and it was implemented by Administration. The pantie raids ceased shortly thereafter, since my suggestion totally took the forbidden excitement out of the activity.

I took the comprehensive exam in September and passed, along with one other person. The other four students went to pharmacy college. I was absolutely ecstatic! I decided to take an externship in pathology that summer and was assigned to an orthopedic resident who was rotating through pathology. I had the honor of helping inject the knees of All-American football player Alex Karras, who helped us get to the Rose Bowl. I also knew All-American guard Calvin Jones, who lived across the hall from me in the Quad Dorm. Calvin died in an airplane crash a few years later. His number was retired, as was Karras's.

The second year started and with Rosemarie's nurturing and my sensual needs somewhat fulfilled by my young wife, I was able to study effectively. After placing 112th out of 116 the first year, I jumped ninety places in my class standing the second year.

I had done extremely well in my psychiatry clerkship, and the second summer I remained in Iowa City to take an externship in psychiatry with Paul Huston, M.D. I was well liked by the Department of Psychiatry faculty and decided to go into that field. I had finally found an area where I excelled and which I enjoyed immensely. By this time I had seriously begun to question my desire to be a medical missionary as I began to understand myself better.

In the third and fourth years the stress of medical school continued but was significantly less. I began to enjoy school and was no longer fearful of my professors. I was a terrible "klutz" in surgery, obstetrics-gynecology, urology, and orthopedics but did very well in internal medicine, neurology, and psychiatry. My professors in the former subjects knew I was going into psychiatry and somewhat overlooked my clumsiness when it came to physical procedures such as suturing.

At the end of the third year, each student was required to spend the summer with a general practitioner, as his assistant. I found the summer enjoyable clinically but found day and night calls and emergencies seven days a week nearly unbearable. I knew then that I would never consider general practice and finalized plans to go into psychiatry in the fourth year. I informed the EUB church that I had decided not to be a medical missionary and signed a note agreeing to repay the loan after graduation over a period of years.

All this time my parents had been telling the world their son was going to be a medical missionary. They drove to Iowa City for graduation not knowing of my revised plans. I got my M.D. and Rosemarie got her B.A. in early child development. We still didn't have a car and my parents helped us move to Broadlawns Polk County Hospital in Des Moines, where I would start a rotating internship. My father was "shattered" when he heard I was going into psychiatry. I don't believe he ever forgave me. It didn't matter to me. I stood up to his and Mother's arguments. I saw my father as a weak, controlling, unhappy person whom I no longer feared in any way. I didn't like being around him, but I wasn't cruel to him.

At Broadlawns I was paid ninety dollars plus a room over the furnace area in the back part of the hospital for Rosemarie and myself. Five of my classmates were also interning there. The internship was very stressful, as we had a great deal of responsibility at this charity hospital, which did not have a formal residency training program at the time. We had access to a senior surgical resident from another program in the city and a Hispanic family practice resident. I was fortunate not to have had many surgical or OB procedures that were emergencies. However, my first delivery there was a breech. I was relieved to have the family practice resident in the room with me, but at the crucial moment he said, "Good-bye, Walter; it's time for Perry Como," and left me alone. It was a strain but everything came out OK.

After graduation from medical school, we all felt we knew everything about medicine, but the internship brought a good deal of that pompousness into proper perspective. I also realized we knew a great deal about obscure and rare illnesses but not too much about how to treat the common cold!

Rosemarie had gotten pregnant during my fourth year in medical school and had been taken care of by the senior resident in OB/GYN. One night I was on call and Rosemarie went into labor. A friend covered me while Rosemarie and I went to Iowa Methodist Hospital, where Garrett Laughton Turke was born! I had mixed feelings about being a father at first, but I realized that I was not like my father and that I had learned a lot about what not to do from him.

Life was hard during the internship. We had very little money and still no car yet. We had to walk a mile to the supermarket with a shopping cart even in the winter. We were glad to leave Des Moines. I looked at residencies, but the academic ones all paid very little, so I decided to choose one where we would not have to struggle quite so hard.

My first year of residency training in psychiatry took place in Norwich State Hospital in Connecticut. The residency paid more than many, and at $6,000 a year this salary was a great deal more than I had been making. It was also near Rosemarie's parents and my uncles and aunts near the ocean. Rosemarie and I were given a comfortable apartment to use in the employees' building.

The program was accredited and affiliated with Yale University School of Medicine and the Institute of Living, a renowned private retreat hospital that had its own residency training program. Visiting faculty from both places came weekly, but the foreign residents did not avail themselves of the opportunity, so another American graduate and I had all the time with them. This provided a solid basis for learning diagnostic psychiatry and psychodynamics.

While in Des Moines, we had purchased our first car, a Ford Ranch wagon, stripped down, and we drove to Connecticut with the car loaded clear to the roof. It contained all our personal belongings and was a sight to behold, particularly with an M.D. sticker on the bumper.

I was given the assignment of running the chronic women's ward and (with a copy of Bulfinch's *Mythology*) diligently went about my duties. I soon fell prey to an elderly schizophrenic woman who grabbed my testicles and squeezed them so hard that I screamed. No one had warned me, as was the custom. Apparently she had been doing this for ten years with the first-year residents! A perverse sort of welcome wagon, it seemed.

Life in Norwich was good, and I enjoyed being a full-time resident psychiatrist. I ran one of the last insulin coma treatment wards in the country. Ultimately I decided it was the togetherness and comradery that helped the patients recover rather than the insulin. We also did electroconvulsive therapy and "depatterning," which was being tried as an experiment at the time. The theory behind this therapy was to give frequent electroconvulsive treatments to regress the patient to a childhood state, to the point of being in a diaper, and then "reparent" him with the doctors and nurses being surrogate parents. I tried this with a young schizophrenic patient who had the delusion of being a Gestapo officer and went about the ward doing "Sieg Heils." After his "depatterning" he, unfortunately, returned to the same state he had been in before the "therapy."

One of the staff psychiatrists had paid a belly dancer to come to a patient's party to perform. As the clinical director and the staff psychiatrist commented about the dancer's physical attributes I made a self-righteous comment about the inappropriateness of this activity. I was still judgmental and saw the world as black and white.

Psychoanalytic psychotherapy was the elite therapy (in terms of prestige), and I read all the works of Sigmund Freud,

Karl Abraham, Sandor Ferenczi, Wilhelm Reich, Theodore Reich, and others. My mentors, particularly the ones from Yale, helped me to be a rather good therapist in my first year.

I had an offer to spend my second and third years of training at the Institute of Living in Hartford and was interviewed by the most prominent psychiatrist in the country at the time, Francis Braceland, who had been APA president, consultant to the State Department, and a rear admiral in the Naval Reserve. I stood in awe before this great man in his large office, with plaques and awards covering every square inch of each wall as well as the ceiling. I have tried to emulate him in my own academic office but haven't been able to do the ceiling! I was accepted at the institute, but the stipend was half of what I was earning and I had to decline.

I noted instead that the Mental Health Institute at Cherokee, Iowa, paid $12,000 per annum and was affiliated with the University of Iowa and that my psychotherapy teachers would be graduates of the Menninger School of Psychiatry. Rosemarie and I decided to move again.

While in Iowa, I had a great deal of individual supervision of ongoing psychotherapy cases and was the only resident presenting my psychotherapy process notes to the entire staff and consultants for three hours every Friday morning for two years. I found this a wonderful and yet trying experience. My emotions and foibles were being placed under the microscope for all to see and analyze. It was a wonderful growth experience; my judgmental attitudes improved, and I began to see the "grays" in life rather than a black-white dichotomy.

During this time, Cindy Lee Turke was born. The labor was difficult, and she had a slightly misshapened cranium for a time and a facial hemangioma, which gradually disappeared. Unlike Garrett, who was always well behaved and affectionate, she appeared to be temperamental, not as affectionate, and more independent in her ways. I loved her as much as my firstborn. I enjoyed her assertiveness, as I had locked up my own.

I was a very good resident, enjoying training, and felt well prepared for my future practice. Our family did not socialize much with other residents. Rosemarie and I did not know how to play cards, didn't dance, didn't converse well, and had poor social skills, since they had never been taught to us. Also, my baseball swing wreaked havoc with my golf game, a serious social handicap for any future physician.

Anchors away! I received orders in the summer of 1960 to report for active duty at the U.S. Naval Hospital in Portsmouth, Virginia. I was very pleased, as I had never lived in the South before and I was proud of my two stripes as a lieutenant, the equivalent of an army captain. There were five other psychiatrists there: one from Menninger, one from Harvard, one from Georgetown, one from Columbia, and one from Chicago. One was gay and rather effeminate, but we all cared for and respected him. At that time, when it was discovered that a recruit had lied about being gay, he would have to wear green fatigues with a yellow stripe down the back and was sent to the Marine Corp brig in Norfolk to await discharge papers. The marine guards carried whips.

We were all reserve officers except our captain, who was a friendly and kind southern gentleman who frequently relied on us to make the difficult decisions. The admiral would phone him at 8:00 A.M. sharp every morning, and our captain would always answer the phone, "Yes, ma'am," in a high-pitched, feminine-sounding voice. The admiral did not like it, but the behavior continued. I was assigned the responsibility for taking care of the officers admitted to the naval hospital for psychiatric reasons. I was also in charge of outpatient psychiatry for officers' wives and dependents and took my turn in evaluating and discharging service seamen who were having serious difficulties in their first six months of duty.

I treated a Marine Corps master sergeant who had PTSD. I hypnotized him, telling him he was back in Iwo Jima and to talk about what happened there. He told about marines taking heads from Japanese bodies for target practice and the gold from officers' teeth. He talked about navy seamen packing hamburger around dry ice and feeding it to seagulls so that they would explode in midair. This was considered fun! After reliving these memories and being aware of them in his consciousness, he improved greatly.

One of my patients, the wife of a USMC officer, would drink

a little too much and get through to my admiral at 2:00 or 3:00 A.M., demanding that I be given better quarters, as the psychiatry department was based in WW I barracks on the hospital grounds.

I loved the navy and Virginia. We visited Williamsburg, Yorktown, Jamestown, Richmond, Monticello, and a host of famous Civil War historic sites while we were there. The Officers' club at Virginia Beach was exquisite. I used to go far out on the sandbars to jump the waves immediately after a storm. After leaving the navy, I read an article on sharks and how they come closer to shore in such weather. One morning I was ready to dive into the water when suddenly a large dorsal fin appeared twenty feet from me. I realized it was a great white and that I had come terrifyingly close to being a seafood snack!

The executive officer of the hospital did not like psychiatrists too much and tried to make our lives difficult. We psychiatrists and our wives developed a support group. The men drank scotch together every Wednesday night while the wives discussed other issues. This helped us survive. It was also the first time I learned how to drink.

The commanding officer at the U.S Naval Hospital was Rear Adm. Hubert Van Peenen. We had the utmost respect for this wonderful man, who had been a prisoner in a Japanese prison camp. Once he said to me, "Dr. Turke, I'll give you two grapefruits to put under your naval tunic so you can nurture all my officers."

I suggested on one occasion to Admiral Rickover that he ought to have psychiatrists in his nuclear subs. He said, "Dr. Turke, then the men would find out they had problems."

I was promoted to lieutenant commander while on active duty and given leave time to attend a meeting of the Psychoanalytic Society in Los Angeles to pay tribute to Franz Alexander, one of the most prominent psychoanalysts of our time, as well as a great teacher, on his seventieth birthday. I took the train from Portsmouth to LA, as I feared flying at the time. I had to spend several nights sleeping in the LA bus depot because I couldn't afford a hotel room. I spent my cash reserves one night to watch Sammy Davis, Jr., in the world-famous Cocoanut Grove. The bus station provided enough aberrations of the human character to fill a psychiatric encyclopedia.

I decided to leave the navy after I completed my two years of active duty but did so with some measure of regret. I decided instead that I wanted to go to LA to develop a private practice to take care of movie people. It was the movies, in part, that had helped me survive my childhood.

One of my final memories before leaving the navy concerned a black petty officer who came to see me one day feeling very depressed. He had been raised in the South and seemed uncomfortable sharing his problems with a white man. Although he denied feelings of suicide, I wanted to hospitalize him. I spent a long time talking with him about his life and offered to see him daily. He did not return until two weeks later. He was DOA, having killed himself with rat poison. I later learned he had two wives who had found out about each other. My analysis of how I failed him included being too warm and friendly and spending too much time with him. He was not accustomed to this behavior from southern whites and I believe he felt he could not trust me because of it. It robbed him of his anger, and his suspiciousness had increased. He could not conceive of a white man caring for him.

My memories of the navy would not be complete without a visit to the officers' locker room. One day I entered and a portly lieutenant commander, a radiologist, emerged from the shower and stood in front of the mirror completely nude. He had not seen me enter and that I was observing him. He looked in the mirror and said: "Mirror, mirror on the wall—who is the fairest of them all? You are! You are! You are!" (in a high-pitched feminine voice). He then turned around and saw me, the psychiatrist, watching him! Very humiliating!!

On days that I am feeling low, I come out of the shower (in front of the mirror) and scream, "You are! You are!" —then I feel better. . . .

Chapter 4

I concluded my obligation to the navy in August of 1962. Rosemarie and I had talked about going to LA for some time, mainly because of the opportunities, the weather, and the recreational facilities. Getting away from our parents was added motivation. Three thousand miles seemed a comfortable distance from them.

I interviewed for a job at a new psychiatric hospital in the San Fernando Valley that was about to open called Madre de Vida (Mother of Life). The medical director was to have been a prominent psychoanalyst from Boston who was interviewing for a clinical director. The job paid $15,000. I went to Boston in my dress blues with two and a half stripes to meet him. By some twist of fate, the man said I reminded him of his son, who was also a lieutenant commander. He quizzed me on a variety of clinical topics and hired me on the spot.

The hospital was built in Tarzana, California, being financed by a group of Beverly Hills businessmen. Tarzana was so named because Edgar Rice Burroughs (creator of Tarzan) and his family lived there. I got to know them quite well after we moved to California. Tarzana was over the hill about twenty minutes by freeway from Beverly Hills and UCLA. What no one had bothered to tell me was that there was already an established psychiatric hospital in Van Nuys and referring psychiatrists in the area had been offered stock in that hospital when it was learned there was to be a new hospital opening up. Also, the Boston analyst who had interviewed me had cancer of the prostate that wasn't responding well to therapy, so he decided not to come to LA.

The entire staff had been hired in advance of my arrival, so I had not been party to the interviewing process. I did have the opportunity to hire a recent psychiatric graduate from Wayne State University who was black. Unfortunately, this didn't work out, since I had underestimated the degree of racial prejudice in

LA at the time. People of certain religious groups didn't want to have a physical done by a black psychiatrist and openly said so. Religion and bigotry seemed a contradiction somehow. I felt anger at their prejudice, which harmed a caring, skilled young man.

Some rather prominent patients came to our hospital, which was modern and open. By open, I mean no locked units. One male patient kept deserting from the hospital, so I told him that if he did it again, I would not readmit him. He escaped again and I kept my word. He climbed to the top of the Capitol Records Building in Hollywood and told the police he would jump if I didn't let him back in the hospital. I informed him via the police that I would not readmit him.

The next two hours were difficult for me, but I learned that he had come down and subsequently was hospitalized at Cedars-Sinai Psychiatric Unit. Two months later the patient's psychiatrist called me to say that my refusal to readmit him was the turning point of his beginning to get well.

Unfortunately, many of the referring physicians in the area preferred a closed hospital because they felt it provided more security for their acutely disturbed patients. The hospital continued to lose significant money and was eventually turned into a nursing home when we were unable to turn the finances around.

I moved my patients to Woodview Hospital and opened a private office on Topanga Canyon Boulevard in Woodland Hills on the road to Malibu Beach, near where actors Burt Ward (Robin from *Batman*), Barbara Hershey (known as Barbara Seagull in the sixties), and David Carradine and numerous writers and other celebrities lived. Linda Ronstadt used to sing in a pub on the hill in her micro-miniskirt. George "Goober" Lindsey lived at 6020 Shirley in Tarzana along with his wife. They were to become our friends.

I had the good fortune of having the daughter of a very famous songwriter walk into my office on her own. With my help she got well, and she told her father and her friends about me. I soon had a full "Hollywood practice." I also kept working with a middle-aged chronic schizophrenic man who was very wealthy and wanted me to see him five times a week. My practice was so successful that first year, I wound up with an IRS field audit. My accountant told me it wasn't because they felt I had done anything wrong, but because they wished to get data on various medical specialists and I had been more successful in my first year than most psychiatrists.

I had studied long and hard for my boards in psychiatry during my stint with the navy and took them as soon as I was eligible. I feared the neurology part the most. I had memorized A. B. Baker's syllabus in neurology down to the fine print. I felt I had done well in my psychiatry orals, but then I came at last to neurology. Imagine my surprise when the examiner turned out to be A. B. Baker himself. I quoted him down to the fine print, and he was completely impressed!

I was supposed to take my boards in New Orleans, so I carried textbooks along to study the night before. I was so anxious, though, I couldn't concentrate, so I walked the few blocks to Bourbon Street for a drink in a small bar I found there. Not long after sitting down, I felt a hand on my thigh.

"Will you buy me a drink?" a young woman asked me. Southern hospitality, it seemed.

"Sure," I replied, always eager to make a friend.

The bartender said, "Fifteen dollars."

"Will you me buy another one?" she said, obviously smitten with my good looks.

"No," I answered and she disappeared, having found some flaw in my character, it seemed. The same scene was repeated with three other women, except that I refused all of them the first time. They left immediately, having discovered the same shortcomings in my personality as had their enterprising sister.

"Do you want to sleep with my twelve-year-old sister?" was another come-on as I left the bar.

I said, "No thanks," and went back to the hotel to sleep!

When Rosemarie and I first came to LA, we had purchased a small ranch-style house in Woodland Hills for about thirty-six thousand dollars. The realtor told me this was his first experience with having to get four mortgages on a house. We had saved only

$2,000 in the navy for moving expenses and a down payment on a house.

The success of my practice soon allowed us to move to posh East Woodland Hills, south of the Ventura Freeway. Prior to that we had been north of the freeway. Our new place was located in a former orange grove. It cost us $85,000 and had six orange trees, two lemon trees, a fig tree, and numerous tall palm trees and banana trees. The outdoor deck was suitable for dancing and looked out over a large heated pool. I also purchased a gold Cadillac Eldorado for myself and a blue Camaro for Rosemarie. I wore Brooks Brothers suits to the office, at least until the late sixties, when the hippie movement and the sexual revolution led my patients and me to don Nehru jackets and Egyptian jewelry and love beads. I bought a new wardrobe of Nehru jackets at Sy Devore's in Hollywood, and a month later the fad ended.

Our "neighbors" in the area included Lee J. Cobb, Chuck Connors, and Robert Culp and comedian Bud Abbott of Abbott and Costello. I tried to get my children to collect autographs when they went trick-or-treating at Halloween. They didn't share my enthusiasm and refused. Lucille Ball's makeup man lived across the street and once made me up as Fu Manchu for a costume party. Across the street lived actress Lisa Ware, whose sister was actress Debra Pagett. They knew Gov. Ronald Reagan and actor Richard Harris very well. I had always wanted to meet Harris since I had seen him on the New York stage as King Arthur in *Camelot,* and I enjoyed his two records "The Yard Went On Forever" and "A Tramp Shining." His music seemed to capture the spirit of the sixties for me, especially my then-favorite song, "MacArthur Park."

Everyone got caught up in the sixties, some more than others. Everyone wanted to live a simple life of freedom and meaning, burning the credit cards and getting rid of luxuries and things that reeked of opulence. Many people got into drugs, including marijuana and "acid." I tried marijuana once in the home of a UCLA psychiatrist. I got warm and mellow; my wife went into a panic and almost went through a glass door trying to escape some unknown terror by jumping into the swimming pool. I never tried any other drugs.

Free love was everywhere and there were parties where the car keys were all put in the center of the table and the keys you got were the keys of the person you were supposed to go home with. My wife and I never participated, but I certainly did in my sexual fantasies. I heard of the exploits of my patients, and it made me envious and brought back memories of my own "deprivations" in this area. Rosemarie remained rather prim and proper, always changing clothes in the bathroom and lacking any real passion during our lovemaking. She also despised my cigar smoking and some of the jokes I shared with her from my patients. In most other ways she was a wonderful wife. I never gave astrology any credence, but Rosemarie was a Libra, iron-fisted with a velvet glove. This appeared partially true. I am a Cancer and this seems to fit me rather well, but it wasn't a very satisfying blend with her. Studies of medical students appear to indicate that the stresses of medical school lead students who marry to choose nurturing mother or father figures to help them get through. At midlife crisis time they then look for romantic love. For men this often means finding a younger and more sensuous woman.

Rosemarie got pregnant unexpectedly with our third child during this time. She became quite depressed, which only accentuated our difficulties. Our communication, such as it was, broke down even more.

My problems became greater soon after that. I received a phone call via the answering service one night from a young woman who told me it was an emergency and she needed to see me right away. Her name was Ellen. I met her in the office, where she shared with me that she had been seeing a psychiatrist who was helping her through her recent divorce from her husband. She complained that her psychiatrist had propositioned her in the parking lot after her last session with him.

I helped her through the anxiety and anger she had over the incident and gave her the names of three colleagues she could call if she needed more help in the future. I was too smitten with her to ever treat her again. Ellen was the most beautiful woman I had ever seen in my life, to the point where I inwardly trembled whenever I looked at her.

Several months later she called me at the office and asked me if I'd like to have a cup of coffee with her. She said it was "social," not "professional." After some serious soul-searching, I did meet her at a small restaurant near my office. I noticed that all the men in the coffee shop were reacting to her as I was. Before leaving, I asked her out to dinner at a Polynesian restaurant on La Cienega Boulevard. My heart raced when she told me that she liked me very much. The relationship grew from there, and several months later we went away for the weekend to San Diego's Mission Bay, where I experienced a lovemaking and passion that I had never dreamed existed. Later we went to Santa Barbara for a weekend, but President Kennedy was shot while we were there. Our depression was so intense that we returned early to our separate homes. My guilt feelings for having sex outside my marriage were very severe, because my behavior went against all my personal values and religious beliefs. But there was also a feeling of entitlement because of my earlier celibacy.

In spite of my guilt, the relationship lasted nearly seven months. The birth of Tiffanie, our third child, along with Rosemarie's intuition about what was happening, made me feel I must either end the affair or leave my family. I would have left my marriage were it not for the children.

I told Ellen good-bye and in anger she told me I was the last medical specialist she wanted to seduce, having already succeeded with a surgeon, OB/GYN, pediatrician, internist, urologist, and radiologist. It made it easier to leave, although I did not believe her. I felt we really loved each other. Ellen kept calling the house, threatening to harm herself, and we would see each other under these periods of crisis. I would talk her down once a month, and then we always made love. Eventually the phone calls ceased and I knew she had met someone else. I felt extremely sad but greatly relieved. It took six months to even begin to get over the pain.

I got reinvolved with my family. We traveled all over on weekends—to Palm Springs, riding the tram up to the pine forest and the snow fields six thousand feet up, to the Erawan Hotel and to Desi Arnaz's resort in Palm Desert, and up to the Norwegian Village at Solvang, the mission at Santa Barbara, the beaches at

Malibu (surfers), Zuma (family beach now gone nude), Muscle Beach (weight lifters), and Venice Beach ("crazies"), where we saw Wilt Chamberlain of the Lakers playing volleyball. We went to Disneyland, Knott's Berry Farm, and other amusement parks.

Rosemarie took art lessons from Rosemarie Calder, whose husband, Maury, was a movie agent. They invited us over one evening for dinner, and the only other couple there was Ted Turner and Deanna Lund, who was staring in *Valley of the Giants*, a new TV series. Ted and Maury talked business all night while the two Rosemaries chatted about their art and decorating interests and Deanna told me about her "analysis" and Hollywood career.

It was a most forgettable evening, except Ted gave me an autographed baseball for my son, Garry. I didn't feel comfortable with Ted, and it was plain to see he was uneasy with psychiatrists. I didn't know at the time about Ted's great fear that he would die prematurely at fifty-eight, the age at which his father had committed suicide.

About this time I started taking karate lessons. I had a choice of two instructors: Chuck Norris, a relative unknown on Ventura Boulevard in Sherman Oaks, and Bill Ryusaki, in North Hollywood. I wanted a Japanese instructor who could teach me the cultural aspects and the traditions that went with karate. I sometimes have regrets. Perhaps Chuck and I would have been friends and I could have been hired as a "bad guy" in all his films!! Anyway, I took two-hour individual lessons twice a week and two three-hour group lessons a week. After two years of very hard study, I got the *shodan* belt (bottom rung of the black-belt ladder), after going through purple and brown belts first.

My first opportunity to put my skills to practical use was wasted, however. In Hawaii, Rosemarie and I came back from the beach at the Royal Hawaiian Hotel and came upon a burglar breaking into our suitcase in our room. As a new purple belt, I feared hurting him and "froze." The first rule of black belts is to run away rather than hurt someone. In this case the thief was in little danger, as he ran down the hall with Rosemarie chasing him!

While visiting the island of Hawaii with the Southern California Psychiatric Society, Rosemarie and I stopped at the Japanese house of my karate instructor's parents. Bob Stoller from

UCLA, a renowned author and researcher in sexual perversions, was with us. One psychiatrist had apparently invited a patient of his, a transvestite, to come along. He had used the women's rest rooms with all of our wives, and none of us knew until we were in the airport on the way home. Bob Stoller's young kids, having been more observant than the adults, told us "She's a he!" Bob and I were both embarrassed.

The evening when I was awarded the *shodan* belt, I had to stand at attention in a karate stance while the other black belts "congratulated" me by striking me in the stomach with their fists. I then got the belt from the star of the TV series *The Virginian.*

Some years later, in January, 1981, at about four in the afternoon, I was in a large square outside the Lima Sheraton in Peru looking at some souvenirs to buy for my children. I watched uneasily as three toughs approached; dispersing left, right, and center, they got closer. The one from the left went after the wallet in my back pocket. As he did, I hit him with a downward block with my left hand; I heard his wrist crack as he went down. I shoved my right elbow into the lower ribs of the man behind me to the right. He groaned as his ribs cracked and he fell to the pavement. The front tough punched out my front tooth as I kicked him in the groin and put him down. I picked up my tooth and said, "*No mueve usted or esta muerto* [don't move or you're dead]!"

The rest of the day I hid in my hotel room, and I flew into Quito, Ecuador, where I paid a dentist $200 to put my tooth back in temporarily until I could get back to my own dentist.

We had a memorable party at our house in Woodland Hills one evening. Bill Rusaki dug a hole and roasted a pig for our friends. There was Japanese food and entertainment and a karate demonstration. I broke some wooden boards for the first time. A dentist friend of mine and I demonstrated *kumite,* which consists of sparring strikes to lethal areas that are stopped one inch before making contact. Most actual strikes are deadly, unlike karate choreographed in the movies. Inadvertently in the excitement, and I think the dentist had had some sake, we kicked each other in the groin. Fortunately for me, I was wearing my steel cup; the dentist was not!

Watching karate on TV these days, I find it amusing to see

the actors wearing gloves and shoes, since we were trained in bare hands and feet. Children should not take karate until they have muscular control, sometime in late adolescence. They should take judo instead, which is a more gentle art and closer to wrestling.

We joined the Woodland Hills Country Club, and occasionally I had the good fortune to golf with several of the Los Angeles Dodgers pitching staff: Sandy Koufax, Don Drysdale, and Ron Perranoski, as well as members of the cast of the *Untouchables* TV series who also golfed there. We attended the Deb-Star Ball, sitting next to Telly Savalas and Phyllis Diller. We went to Dick Van Dyke's home in Encino. His garden was immaculate, as evidenced by the rake marks visible in the dirt over the entire yard. Three cars were parked there: an Eldorado, a Mercedes, and the car from *Chitty Chitty Bang Bang*.

The Watts riots occurred and the violence frightened our community. During this time there were rumors on the radio and in the papers that blacks were going to terrorize affluent neighborhoods in the valley, so I bought a Beretta pistol and had the children lie on the floor at night when they slept. Many of the houses in our block were being burglarized. I recall a cop from the Los Angeles Police Department telling me if I ever shot a burglar in the backyard, I had better drag the body into the house to avoid prosecution.

Rosemarie would frequently shop at this one supermarket early Sunday mornings near our house. Robert Culp was usually there, too, always wearing dark glasses but looking around, apparently wishing to be recognized. At the time he was starring in the TV series *I Spy* with Bill Cosby. Rosemarie pretended not to recognize him, which appeared to distress him.

We went to dinner at the Sportsman's Lodge, where we could catch our own trout and then have it for dinner. One night the entire Cartwright family (including Michael Landon) from the *Bonanza* series was there. It was fun seeing movie stars in person, and most of the discussions that were held socially were about "show biz."

"Goober" (George Lindsey) from the old *Andy Griffith Show* came over one Saturday for a pool party. He took my oldest daughter on his knee and sang to her while perched on the diving board of our pool.

Later Goober went into the den to study his TV script. There, he came face to face with our pet regal python, which we were raising. The snake was by then fifteen feet long and had progressed from eating live rats to rabbits. We had built a large cage for it with a tree and a baby bathtub and a large heat light. Goober vowed never to return to our house, but after some coaxing he stayed, playing his new record over and over again until midnight!

When we left LA in June 1971, we gave our python to the LA zoo and had a family picture taken for the zoo bulletin (holding the snake of course).

One evening Rosemarie and I went to a pool party in Sherman Oaks at the home of a dentist friend of ours. His neighbors were Jack Webb, Julie London, Steve Allen, and Roger Williams. An obstetrician threw me in the pool with all my clothes on, including my watch and wallet, etc. I later returned the favor before I left.

When we got home later that night I discovered that I had lost the key to our house, so I was forced to climb the wall to our backyard to retrieve a hidden key, whereupon our German shepherd attacked me because she couldn't catch my smell. She finally recognized my voice just in time to keep her from dismembering me.

There seemed to be no end to the entertainment opportunities surrounding us in Los Angeles, so that time in our lives was full of vivid memories.

Chapter 5

During my years of practice in LA and Michigan, I saw many patients and was able to use that experience to help more and more people solve or at least minimize their mental health problems. A few patients stick out from the crowd.

I received a call from an "entertainer" requesting an appointment to see me. On the afternoon of the appointment I received a call saying that she was waiting on the corner of a street three blocks away and that I needed to pick her up so she could get to my office. She had apparently hitched a ride to that point. She informed me that she was a stripper at the Pink Pussy Cat, a famous establishment in Hollywood. I asked her to please call a cab, but she said she didn't have any money with her.

Grudgingly I went to pick her up. As I stopped the car, she opened her coat wide—she was wearing nothing underneath! I was embarrassed walking with her in the parking lot and through the lobby of the professional building! She had been pressured to see me by a friend who was a patient of mine. This woman had no real interest in therapy and I didn't accept her as a patient.

One of my patients was starring in a very popular TV series. He would come to the professional building an hour early and drink coffee, talking to everyone who sat near us, telling everyone what a wonderful psychiatrist I was. I suggested that I felt uncomfortable with this behavior and that perhaps he was feeling guilt over being angry with me for some reason. Most patients tend to feel a complex blend of love-hate for their psychiatrists. The reasons often have to deal with transference, painful interpretations of problems, envy, and gratitude for the nurturing and understanding they were receiving.

I was in the middle of a session with a patient in my office one afternoon when the phone rang. The interruption was unusual, since I had left instructions with the answering service that I wasn't to be disturbed during office hours. (Since I preferred to work without a receptionist, my calls were routed through the service.) When I answered the phone, the operator said she had an emergency on the line for me. I heard a soft, gentle voice speaking when I was connected to the caller.

"Dr. Turke, I'm a second-year UCLA medical student and I'm very depressed and want to kill myself. Can you see me right away? I'm desperate for help."

"Yes, of course. I'll back up the rest of my afternoon schedule," I said.

I gave the woman instructions for getting to my office, then went to the patient sitting in the waiting room.

"I hope you won't mind a slight delay. I have a serious emergency coming," I said.

"That's okay, Dr. Turke. I'll be right here until you're finished," he replied.

I was just finishing up with the patient already in my office when I heard the chime ring on the door to the waiting room and went to meet the patient. I was surprised to see a muscular, heavy woman standing close to six feet tall and weighing maybe two hundred pounds. She looked to be in her late thirties. Her voice was gruff and deep as she introduced herself. She was certainly nothing like the feminine person I had been expecting due to the voice I had heard over the phone.

"I'm Lauri, the UCLA medical student," she said angrily as we entered my office.

"Are you sure you're the one who called?" I said. "You sound a lot different in person."

There was no answer.

"Are you sure you're a medical student?" I continued.

No answer.

"I'm going to have to call your dean to check," I pressed her.

"Don't touch that phone, you shit, or you'll be sorry!" she said.

"OK, but I need to know who you really are."

There was silence for nearly five minutes while she continued to stare at me angrily, deep in thought. Finally she spoke. "I'm married to ——— [and then she mentioned the brother of a famous musician]. We're having marital problems. I think he's been seeing other women. I lied so you would see me right away."

"I' m not sure I'm going to accept you as a patient. I value honesty, and I have to trust my patients in order to treat them."

"You're making me goddamn angry, you fucking bastard!" she yelled. "I'm lonely and I want you to fuck me right now on your couch or I'll kick your ass!"

"Are you serious? How could I possibly keep you as a patient when you are attempting to frighten me, make me angry, and then ask me to do something that violates my value system? I'm going to have to ask you to leave right now," I said.

"You fucking fairy, are you a little light on your feet or something? Maybe you like young boys instead? You'd better fuck me now or you'll be goddamned sorry!"

I got to the waiting room door and asked the patient I had talked to earlier to call the police.

"John, emergency! Call the police from the dentist's office next door!"

Lauri, the "student" grabbed me by the back of my collar, pulled me back into my office, and threw me into my chair.

"Fucking bastard!" she shrieked.

She began trashing my office. She kicked over my table, pulled all my books from the shelves and threw them all over the room, plucked the paintings from the walls and tossed them around, and pitched the phone against a wall. She then attempted to strike me several times, but I blocked her punches with karate moves. I was glad my instructor, Bill Rusaki, had taught me how to defend myself even when sitting down. Apparently frustrated with being unable to hit me, she backed away. I sat immobile in my chair without saying a word. I didn't wish to have a physical confrontation with her at any price. I'd rather have my office damaged than harm her or have her sue me. Also, I was so angry I was afraid I'd inadvertently hurt her severely, so I became overly passive.

After what seemed like an eternity the police finally arrived. As they were coming into the office she threatened to hit me again.

"What's going on, doctor?" one of the officers said while grabbing her.

“Officer, this woman asked me for an emergency consultation. You can look at me and my office. She did it because I wouldn’t make love with her. I’ll press charges, but in the meantime you should take her to USC/LA County Medical Center for psychiatric screening.”

The officer handcuffed the woman and took her away, surprisingly without any comment from her.

“Take care, Doc, ” said the policeman with a smile.

I surveyed the damage to my office. There were cigar ashes all over the place, books everywhere, two broken picture frames, two shattered vases, and a torn shirt.

The police called back about an hour later and told me the woman had been admitted to the USC/LA County Medical Center. When I contacted UCLA, they said they didn’t have a medical student with the name or matching the description I gave them. I doubted her claim to be the wife of the musician but if indeed she was, it was doubtful they ever made beautiful music together. It appeared that there might be dire consequences for him if he failed to perform.

I was on call for psychiatry for the LA County Medical Society when I received a page stating that there was an emergency request at an address in North Hollywood. I got into my car at about 10:00 P.M. and drove out to see the person. I found the address, but just as I was about to pull in the driveway I was preceded by a liquor store delivery truck that dropped off two fifths of vodka with a woman at the door of the house. I entered the front room of the place and spotted the liquor on the table next to an open triple-X porno magazine. The woman said, “Let’s party!” and I said, “I’m getting the hell out of here!”

Chapter 6

In a profession such as mine there are always unusual people to meet. There are, however, patients who stick out from the rest because of the intensity of pathology or the uniqueness of their personality. One such distinctive individual was a UCLA art instructor who bartered paintings for therapy. The artwork was of such a high quality and psychological intensity that I hung the pictures in my office. Jonah's father had died when he was very young, and he had a great deal of inner conflict with his Jewish mother, whom he perceived as controlling and domineering. He was an only child. His mother lived in a small house in West LA and was always asking him for one of his paintings. He told me, "I always paint them so large they won't fit into her house." I treated him from 1963 through 1967.

The paintings he gave me in return for his services were:

1. One of a spiderlike man dissecting a nude woman. It was very shocking, with a great deal of red paint depicting blood and violence.
2. One painted when Jonah broke up with his girlfriend, who frequently betrayed him sexually with other men. This time he felt she had left him for good. The painting was full of dark blues, with a shadowy figure who appeared to be "falling apart" sitting alone behind an empty table. Jonah was very depressed when he painted this. The table was bare, without food or drink. (The nurturance was gone!)
3. One painted after Jonah's girlfriend, who was working as an extra in some movies and was extremely attractive, came to see me, at his request, to tell me that she didn't want to return to him. He appeared very angry when I told him, both at her and also at me since he apparently felt I should have been able to save their relationship. This

painting was full of dark colors, but mostly browns. In the center one can perceive a head with an open mouth threatening aggressively as if to bite. In other words, "I'll get you, you SOB!" I have this painting in my den.

4. One painting after Jonah and I worked through his feelings about his girlfriend, his anger at her for abandoning him, plus his hostility towards me for not bringing them back together. We also discussed his emotional dependency on me. He began to feel better as he recognized that his pain might very likely have been even greater if the relationship with her had continued. He began to express a great deal of warmth toward me, seeing me as the brother he always wished he had and as the father he never knew. The painting that resulted showed two men standing close to each other, with the taller man having his arm around the smaller. If you look closely, you can see the smaller man has a huge erect penis that almost extends into his mouth!
5. One painted after, when I was engaging in *kumite* with my Japanese instructor, I "inadvertently" kicked him in the groin and my toe was severely sprained, hitting his steel cup, making it necessary to wear a slipper to the office and elevate my leg. Jonah became enraged that I was taking karate and was very jealous of my karate instructor. This painting showed a reptilian creature swooping down on two karate black belts wearing their "Gi's." One karate man was attempting to run away, obviously in great terror. The reptilian creature makes a "don't be afraid" gesture to this karate man (me), but kills the other (my instructor). The painting has a border of Japanese symbols and my office number, 450, in the upper left corner. I have this painting in my bedroom.
6. The last painting, done near the end of his therapy. It shows a beautiful Japanese landscape with soft colors while a strong and powerful Japanese man surveys his domain. There is a large sun in the sky, and the face in the sun represents me benevolently and caringly watching him. I have this painting in my living room.

7. Lithographs done in midtherapy:
   a. *The Fishing Boat.* There is a small and frail figure sitting on one side of the boat holding a small fish (representing a penis); on the other side of the boat is a large Viking-like woman standing tall and muscular with a large fish. Jonah stated that this picture represented him and his mother.
   b. *The Stage.* The scene is the theater. Onstage is a bed with an arrow pointing under it. Jonah stated that his dead father was under the bed. Onstage, in the corner, a woman is pulling a small boy/man into corridors where there are monsters (representing homosexuality). In a theater box overlooking the stage I sit, again watching him.
   c. *The Diner.* Jonah sits alone in one of the chairs in the diner. The woman behind the counter is seen taking the food away from him. He is not only completely alone, but he has no nourishment. In one of the corner booths I sit watching him.

Chapter 7

Perhaps the most challenging of all my patients was a schizophrenic man by the name of Ben who was forty-five at the time I began a nine-year association with him. Ben was tall, lean, and balding, with sunken eyes and false teeth. He was a very intelligent man with an engineering degree from UCLA. He was Jewish, with the tendency toward snobbery that comes from great wealth, often manifesting itself in such statements as that he didn't want to be like the "common man." He was the only male child but had a younger sister he was very close to.

Ben's father was a self-made multimillionaire who was always working and heavily involved with his business ventures. Opinionated and assertive, he spent little time with his son. The man at seventy-five was still going into his office regularly and remained sexually active up into his eighties.

Ben's mother was a California aristocrat who was very nurturing to her children. Ben often fought bouts of depression when he was younger by talking to his mother. Her death during childbirth while Ben was in college was a severe blow to his stability, and he became profoundly depressed.

Ben was the product of his parents' conflicting personalities. His father put extreme pressure on him with high expectations for achievement while his mother coddled and protected him.

The final blow to Ben's sanity came when he was in the navy. His father married a woman who was obviously both physically and emotionally unlike Ben's mother. The woman had masculine traits and a deep voice and was twenty years younger than Ben's father. She also had a great deal of her own money.

Ben became intensely angry with his father but could find no way to express his feelings. He became psychotic while aboard a navy minesweeper. Against naval regulations he erected an antiaircraft gun aboard the minesweeper he was commanding, being fearful of a Japanese air attack. He was discharged from the navy and spent the next few years just wandering aimlessly around the family estate. During this time he tried to murder his stepmother with a knife and later to castrate himself with a cord. His depression and anger caused him to regurgitate so much gastric juice his teeth rotted and had to be pulled.

I was the fourth psychiatrist Ben had been entrusted to over the years. The first one died of cancer and the second of suicide, which was obviously counterproductive for Ben. Ben often thought that the man may have killed himself just to get away from him. The third psychiatrist was fired after ten years because of a growing conflict with Ben's father.

Ben came into my life shortly after I moved to LA and provided me with a great opportunity both professionally and economically. The Turke family fortune had a lot of minus signs attached to it at the time. I was $50,000 in debt from the loans that had gotten me through college and med school. I had earned $1,800 a year as an intern, $6,000 as a resident, and $8,000 as a navy lieutenant commander for two years. The down payment on the house we bought in Woodland Hills took half the $2,000 savings we had accumulated and had four mortgage loans attached to it. I was just starting up my private practice when I was given the opportunity and the challenge of treating this very psychotic schizophrenic man. I enjoyed the work, spending fifteen to twenty hours a week with him. The fees I was paid for his treatment gave me financial stability until my movie-star practice took off.

While difficult and often torturous, my relationship with Ben provided me with insight and understanding into his mental disorder that many other psychiatrists might never obtain. I took what I learned and applied it to many experiences and patients over the years.

Ben's illness was characterized by a vicious cycle that consisted of an excessive need for love and dependency but a conflicting concomitant fear of people. His anxiety about being close to another person caused him to run away each time his loneliness compelled him to seek the nurturing of another human being. As a consequence his needs were never satisfied.

Ben believed he was bad, ugly, vicious, and dangerous because he felt he had not been loved. This led him to feel intense hostility, coupled with a desire for revenge. This in turn compounded his feelings of guilt and unworthiness. He withdrew, attempted to deny his need for love, and then attempted to change himself so he would not need love. The denied need for love became a tremendous threat, and he modified his thoughts and ego out of a fear of rejection, which was expressed in terms of his distrust of others.

Ben was extremely sensitive and easily hurt. His apathy and emotional shell were created to protect him and the little love he had. He felt hopeless and alone, frequently describing himself as an "empty bag or stomach." Any human contact would tend to arrest the regression and as he was unable to love very much, there was only one thing left to preserve his ego and that was hate. Hate is basically a denied love, a combination of love plus fear. In hating, Ben was able to relate to people, so hate was a good sign from his perspective. He did not feel as much guilt about hate; he felt guiltier about love because love was much more dangerous to him.

Ben and I had an excellent rapport almost from the start because he no doubt had an acute awareness of my genuine liking for him. I attempted to assume a consistent and accepting posture in his treatment, allowing Ben to come as close as he wished, yet recognizing his need to run away and create distance periodically. I was careful not to pursue him, for this would compel him to be unduly anxious.

Ben was never put on the couch, nor was free association used, since this would have made him worse. He needed to look me in the eyes to see if he could trust me. I attempted to be punctual and thoroughly reliable at all times, because anything less would have been construed as a rejection. Ben forgave my mistakes because he perceived my intentions as good and realized I respected him as a person.

An analysis of Ben's unconscious was not being undertaken, as his unconscious was already conscious. I attempted to help Ben repress much of the psychotic material he talked about, which led to some improvement. This was done by constant reference to present reality. Concomitantly I searched for the feelings underlying the content of his communications and responded to them in a way that let him know I understood and was with him. There was very little intellectual interpretation of the content.

I attempted to be honest with Ben at all times and expressed my anger to him appropriately when he provoked it rather than attempting to conceal it, as his parents may have done. I usually explained the reasons for my anger so he understood. He seemed to find this type of honesty refreshing, leading to further trust. I attempted to be thoughtful regarding Ben's great demands on me and attempted to make certain this was not the reason for my anger toward him.

When Ben got to LA after being transferred from an eastern hospital where he had been in residence for ten years, he appeared apathetic and depressed and rarely spoke. About ten days after his arrival, he said, "I don't know what happened; I cracked up and ate all my supper." These were his first words to me.

By this time he had gotten to know me better. I would see him for ten minutes three times a day, as I felt he could not tolerate more contact with me at this time. He would become greatly alarmed if we inadvertently touched each other in the hall or going through doorways During those initial sessions, I told him I understood how sad he was and how he missed his former therapist. Other than such comments, I was largely a listener, although for the first six to eight weeks he spoke very little. His few utterances were such things as: "I'll be killed; this is a pogrom"; "They'll cut it off"; "I don't know who you are"; "Who's paying you? I'll be in the poorhouse"; "You dirty son of a bitch!"; and "You're the greatest hero who ever lived and you admit it."

He found it impossible to sit still in the office, so we would walk the halls together. In time we extended our activities to include walking around the hospital grounds. Sometimes he would run away from me, going down the street, and I would run after him. I would kid him that we would soon both be ready for the Olympics. On one occasion when he had run away, I found him in a local store waiting for me with a package of cupcakes.

As we returned to the hospital, he offered me a cupcake, which I was pleased to accept. We got back to the hospital, soaked from the rain and eating our snack. After this incident, his sadness seemed to leave for a time. Sometimes on our walks he would test me by threatening to eat dirt, jump into a fountain with his clothes on, or strike other patients. I usually responded in a consistent way by telling him that I wouldn't allow it because it would hurt his self-respect.

At the end of the first month of care I began to see him for half an hour at a time, and the following pattern developed. We would spend the first ten minutes or so in my office just talking. His conversations continued to be rambling and incoherent, but I now felt free to interrupt him with reality-oriented questions such as what had he eaten for breakfast, what had he been reading in *Time* magazine, and who had won the local ball game. When his tensions and anxiety would build while we were in the office, we would go to the hospital dining room for coffee and doughnuts. This usually occurred at times when most of the other patients were having breakfast. As soon as we entered the dining room, he would begin to talk in a boisterous way. Sometimes he would declare that I was the greatest hero the world had ever known, but that he refused to have homosexual relations with me. Whenever another patient of mine would offer to replenish my coffee, Ben would either strike at the patient or break the cup. He appeared resentful of any staff member or patient who came to the table. After the session in the dining room, we would take our walk down the street.

In the middle of January, Ben's father called to say that he had received a letter from his son, adding that it was the best he had ever written and the first letter in over a year.

The first thing Ben would do in the morning was look for my car. As soon as I entered the building he would laugh or yell loudly to let me know he was there and ready to talk. At times he tested me by insisting we talk and walk in the usual manner regardless of how heavily it might be raining. Needless to say, we always took our walk.

During the bad weather he would say, "Perhaps the rain will help the grass to grow and become green again."

This was his way of saying that perhaps my interest in him would help him become alive again.

At times he would be late for his hour or even hide. When this occurred, I would play the game with him and seek him out. Usually he would be hiding in the closet of his room or under his bed. Occasionally he would refuse to come to the office and I would respond that treatment was important and I would have him carried by attendants if he would not come of his own choice. Most of the time he would react to this with loud proclamations of hate for me, followed by a great decrease in his general anxiety. On three occasions, however, this procedure led to his hitting me with his fist. When he did I would look angrily at him and growl, "You're pretty damn anxious today. We'll talk more at the same time tomorrow."

Following such an incident, I would drop by his table at lunch for a quick cup of coffee and to say hello.

Madre de Vida Hospital was closed and later became a nursing facility for geriatric patients. As a consequence I moved Ben to a closed-unit psychiatric hospital in Van Nuys.

One afternoon I asked Ben if he would like to leave the hospital and walk to a movie. He said he would enjoy doing so, but halfway there he said he wanted to go by himself. When I told him that he would not be allowed to do that he took off running. I flagged down a police car and they caught him and escorted him back to the hospital. After we got inside he glared at me, screamed that I was a dirty son of a bitch, and kicked me hard in the groin. After I recovered, I told him we would not go out anymore because he was too ill.

Shortly after the incident I began studying my karate in earnest. Later when Ben got well enough he would go to the *dojo* with me and watch the two-hour lessons. Ben was always well-behaved at the *dojo.* The instructor made him bow to him and told him to take off his shoes. Ben was very passive and obedient with the instructor.

On Christmas Day of that year Ben became very agitated and told me, "I was in my mother's belly. My penis was being twisted off."

He threatened suicide and refused medicine because he felt

it was poisoned. This period of upset appeared to be related to his developing greater closeness with me, which he perceived as dangerous, as well as the sadness this time of year seemed to bring him.

Eventually as Ben came to realize that the situation had stabilized, he became less anxious and was heard to tell patients and hospital personnel on various occasions, "Dr. Turke is my best and only friend."

The following week he was able to comment on his father's recent visit, "My father wanted me to be neat, but after Mother died, he married another woman. That is what I do not like. I don't like my father because of jealousy. At his age he's in better shape than I am."

During April, May, and June, Ben demonstrated a good deal of improvement. His pacing and loose verbalizations diminished and he socialized with other patients. He was taken to the theater and movies by the hospital's male director of nursing and did well at these times. He suffered a brief upset in mid-April when the submarine *Thresher* was sunk, because it brought back memories of his time in the navy. He felt guilty and personally responsible for the *Thresher*'s predicament.

During the weeks of September through early October, he became increasingly discontented with the hospital surroundings, saying he was bored. He felt he was in prison and intimated in other ways that he wanted more freedom and responsibility. At this point I will report some of his talks with me in October, to show the nature of our relationship after ten months of therapy.

"I told you I hated you, but I'm too yellow to swing at you. I'm the most hated man in the world. I'm the leader, so they are going to pull it off today," he said.

"I understand how anxious you feel," I said.

There was a short pause, and he said, "I got up early today to look for your car."

"I understand," I replied with a smile.

"What do you do when you have hot nuts for a woman?" he asked.

"It's OK to have strong feelings," I said reassuringly.

"I'm talking to God, my spirit. I'll torture myself for not

slugging you when I should. I'm yellow. I want to slug you because you're trying. I've known you since you were a child. You're not from New York. I shouldn't talk and start pogroms. I have Bob H. His dog licked my face and made me feel like a dog."

This session was characterized initially by warmth closeness, which led to Ben's developing sexual feelings for me. My interpretation about strong feelings was perhaps too direct, and he reacted with anger and guilt, verbalizing that I had licked his face by getting too close.

The following day he said, "I'm not a penis; I'm a nice person. I know a lot of boys who worship their penis when it goes in and out. I'm afraid mine will get too long and stretch off. Maybe I'll grow another one. I'm afraid to fight with people. I should fight them all the time, but I'm yellow. I'm interested in orphans."

"I understand how lonely you feel," I said.

"You feel sorry for me because I don't have a best friend. I can only be best friends with the dead people. I get mixed up. I call you B. [former therapist for ten years] instead of Turke." Then he said to himself, "They don't give a damn as long as they get their money." Then, looking at me, he said, "He's a big shot, yeah, about as big as a trained seal. I'm a seal, too."

He began to make seallike noises, his eyes rather twinkling, and I smiled at him.

"You think you are kind; you're the dirtiest son of a bitch I've ever met and I'd like to choke you," he said.

With that he left his chair and put his hands around my throat. With some difficulty I took a casual puff on my cigar, and Ben released his fingers.

"When do you shit?" he said. "At home, I suppose," he answered himself.

He then returned to his chair and sat down.

"Twenty years ago I was mad at you. We met each other when we were young." Then to himself he said, "Who's your best friend? Your father? His stooges? Yourself?"

He paused, looked at me, and softly whispered to himself, "He is, so touch him," and he reached out his hand to touch mine.

Four days later he sang my praises to me: "You're the greatest hero the world has ever known. You are a psychiatrist using yourself as a man. It's man-to-man. [This was the first time he had referred to himself as a man.] You have nothing to fear because you have a wife and family. Rats, dirty, hungry animals. Rats win because they are English Jews. Dad sent them over; that's why he's my enemy. You are still the greatest hero who ever lived." He looked me in the eyes and said, "I like you . . . ," then quickly whispered to himself, "I should conceal it."

Then, frightened, he said, "I'll get the most painful tortures. I don't even know your name. . . . I've got to stop making a pig of myself."

"It's OK to feel close to me," I said.

"You know what they used to call me? Cocksucker. I went to the U and I've sucked a few. No, I really haven't."

"I understand," I replied.

He smiled and appeared much more relaxed.

By October Ben had improved so much that it was decided to transfer him to another hospital in Westwood next to the UCLA campus that had an open ward and a more fully developed and sophisticated activities program. I drove him there personally, but he was still extremely anxious about the move and hallucinated about rats running in the ceiling of his hospital room.

Shortly after the transfer he said, "I didn't hear any rats running around my bed, so these plans will win." To himself he added, "So this is your victory." Then, looking at me, he continued to whisper, "Abraham Lincoln is good. He's true to his word. I am good. too."

This was the first time he had ever referred to himself as "good."

He then betrayed his ambivalence by adding, " . . . but I am not."

Ben made a good adjustment to the open hospital setting, with a few exceptions. One time he ran off and was found attempting to direct traffic at a busy intersection. On another occasion when he ran off, he was found on a curb, pretending to dive in front of cars as though he were going off a diving board. These incidents followed times when he had been particularly close to me in therapy. He showed progress in play, reading, music appreciation, and various athletic pursuits.

Ben was responsible for my getting contact lenses. One day I took him to Disneyland and while I was watching the entertainment at the Western saloon he wandered off, and I couldn't find him for over an hour. I was afraid to leave the saloon because I thought he might come back there. An hour and a half after Ben disappeared, one of the security guards returned him after I had alerted them to his absence and condition. Apparently, he was easy to spot since he had started to take off all his clothes. I was very angry with him. On the freeway heading back to the hospital I said, "We can't do this again. I can't trust you."

"Dirty bastard!" he screamed at me as he ripped my glasses off and threw them out the window while we were doing seventy miles an hour in the fast lane.

His closeness with me continued, however, and one month later he said, "Dr. Turke, I'm a very sick person. I don't know if you can save me, but don't stop anything you are doing."

Three weeks later he said, "Give me your card so I can put it in my pocket over my heart."

Late in April he said, "I'll never got over people I love and respect dying on purpose because they can't put up with me anymore. I guess they did it to protect me, too, so that I wouldn't get married."

Later that hour he said, "It's a sin, the way I'm ruining my brain. When I think of what I might have been, the grim reality of that depresses me."

He left the hospital in the latter part of June to visit the World's Fair in New York, accompanied by a male nurse and a male occupational therapist (OT), both of whom had taken him out of the hospital on weekends and evenings. He enjoyed the trip immensely, and upon his return he said warily, "I love you, Dr. Turke."

In August he said, "I hate you. . . . I guess that means I love you. Yes, I love you. . . . Do you want me to suck it or just look at it?"

"We can be close friends without sucking each other's penis. But it's OK to have strong feelings," I replied.

Ten days later he said, "You are my beloved friend. I used to think that thinking or saying that meant I was a pervert."

During his stay at the hospital Ben did very well and improved more. He adjusted well to group activities and went out a great deal with his two "specials" to baseball and basketball games, bowling, golfing, and the theater. He always appeared to me to become angry or depressed upon his return to the hospital. However, he had verbalized on many occasions his wish to leave and have a home of his own. It was felt that his condition now permitted such a move, and arrangements were then made with his guardians to purchase a home for him.

After a period of time, he commented regarding his new environment, "This therapy is ideal, but I get so far out it's pathetic. This is like a whole new world. I feel so different and I've got to get used to it. I worry about Dad getting sore at me and taking my money away and making me live like the common man. I'm not your equal; I shouldn't be talking to you. I want to do all the things you do, and when I don't, I get angry. I didn't realize how hard it is to get well. I've been in my own world and haven't wanted to leave it until now."

I began to take Ben to visit my home to interact with my wife and three children. He would swim in our pool and play golf with me at our country club. He would usually "hallucinate" only when I was teeing off! Ben went into one of his catatonic states once when the foursome behind us was comprised of Sandy Koufax, Don Drysdale and Ron Perranoski of the Dodgers, along with Paul Picerni from the *Untouchables* TV series. Ben ceased to move, frozen in place and unable to speak. His right arm was locked in a horizontal posture, and he was unresponsive to any verbal commands. I explained to the men what was happening, and unperturbed, they played on through. Despite these moments, the golf pro at the Woodland Hills Country Club liked me and let me keep bringing Ben onto the course. I also arranged for some very expensive golf lessons with him for Ben.

After a month, Ben began to crave more physical contact with my younger daughter. He enjoyed her touching him and smiling at him when he helped her put a shoe back on. He questioned aloud if she could possibly be his child, to which I commented, "That would be a surprise to me."

He responded to this with a big grin, saying, "I am desperately trying to hang onto you; that's why my golf game is improving, because you are my best friend. We've been friends for twenty-three months, so you are my wife."

After leaving the golf course one particular day, we returned to my house, where he said, "I'll get your wife and then Tiffanie [nine months old at this time] will be deformed."

While we were playing checkers together he stated, "I like you a lot now, but in a minute I'll get mad at you again."

Just before leaving, when he was alone with Tiffanie, he picked her up (I watched from an adjoining room) and began to sing to her; then he tried to help her walk. This was in sharp contrast to the anger he would usually show her. His anger had been a manifestation of his jealousy of her because she got attention from me. He was also envious of her for having healthy parents and the opportunities afforded in her life.

Just before Thanksgiving he said, "I really don't like women; all they want to do is screw. The only woman I could ever love is your wife."

On returning from a visit to his family he said, "I had a real good time, but it feels good to be back home." He then looked me in the eye and said, "You have self-respect and I'm trying to find mine through you." This brought tears to my eyes, which he noticed, and he said, "We've had some intimate moments together, haven't we?"

Early in December my older daughter made an impromptu drawing for Ben and gave it to him. He was visibly pleased, kissing her and asking that his hand be kissed in return.

In the middle of December, I was golfing with Ben when I got dust in my eyes and they began to tear. Ben said, "Oh, God! That makes you a woman. No, you're not human at all. You have so many handicaps that I ought to throw this club at you." Later he said, "I want to apologize for being angry with you. It was my sickness talking."

He arrived at our house early on Christmas Eve in 1964 with an armful of presents for the children and we placed them under the tree. We took him to a neighbor's Christmas party and then returned home for Christmas dinner. After dinner he sang carols and sat on the floor with the children to open their presents. His attention was directed to our younger daughter's rocking horse, which he rode with and without her. He said it was the best Christmas he had experienced in over twenty years and kissed my wife warmly on the cheek when he left.

Several days later in the office he said, "If I think of anything good or admit it, it will disappear. If I admit to any asset, it will soon turn into defeat." Later he said, "People never die; they just leave you and don't tell you where they are." Still later he said, "I'll get mad at you because I'm jealous of you. I wish my balls weighed sixteen pounds, too."

Ben's progress over the years made me optimistic enough to take him along with my wife and three children when we took a vacation tour through the Orient: Japan, Hong Kong, Thailand, and Malaysia. In Bangkok, Thailand, it was 110 degrees when we arrived and we were forced to wend our way through the crowded, foul-smelling market area in order to get to our cab and guide.

Ben took out his dentures and threw them on the ground, and we were forced to wrestle him into the car. At the hotel he proceeded to knock some drinks off a tray as a waiter was passing us in the lobby. In the elevator Ben became catatonic, so my son and I had to carry him into our room.

Rosemarie and the two girls had separate but adjoining rooms on the eighth floor. Ben tried to jump out of the window, but I tackled him and Garrett helped me hold him down. This continued until I was able to give him an injection of haloperidol. We were finally able to release him the next morning. Worn out from our efforts, we still had to watch him very closely, even though he was more exhausted than we were.

I called the American embassy as Ben watched. I told him that I knew he wasn't having a good time, that he was jealous of my children, and that we were going home. I told the official at the embassy that I was a naval reserve lieutenant commander and I needed some marines to help me take care of an ex–navy lieutenant.

Ben interrupted, saying, "It's OK. I want to go through with the trip. I want knockwurst and sauerkraut and then I want to see Thai foot fighting."

I thanked the embassy and told them I no longer needed help, at least for the present. Ben did pretty well the rest of the trip, which took us to Singapore, Hong Kong, and the rest of Thailand. He had one brief catatonic seizure at a Japanese inn near Mount Fuji, but otherwise there were no serious relapses.

We flew everywhere on JAL in the first-class section, stayed in the best hotels, and had guides taking us everywhere in Mercedeses. Ben's trustees had told us to take the children with us and that they would pick up the tab for everything.

Not all of Ben's trips went as smoothly. As he progressed he was allowed to take a vacation to Athens, Greece, with his male nurse and the man's wife, also an R.N. When they got to the King George Hotel, Ben became psychotic and began shouting that he was Aristotle Onassis and that everyone was trying to take his money away.

The nurses called me in the middle of the night just after Rosemarie and I had returned from a three-week tour of the Soviet Union. I told the nurses I would close the office for a week to come help them. The trustees sent me first-class again.

When I got there, the nurses had put Ben in a Greek hospital. I sent them back to the United States and checked into their room at the King George. I saw Ben an hour a day at the hospital. He was on extremely high doses of antipsychotics, was in chains, and looked like he had lost thirty pounds. I began immediately to reduce his medications.

"Thank God you came, Walter!" he said. "You've saved me!"

Ben got better in the next few days, and we flew home a week later.

Ben was always providing me with "entertaining moments." He had season tickets to the Lakers basketball game at the Forum, and I would occasionally be the one to accompany him. On one such trip we went in his brand-new convertible T-Bird. Once at the game Ben demanded to go talk to "Wilt the Stilt" Chamberlain, his favorite, since we often saw him playing volleyball over at Venice Beach.

When I told Ben that his request was not possible he became very angry. Out came his teeth, which I stuffed in my pocket. While I was retrieving his dentures he took off his sport shirt and undershirt and then his pants. The ushers came and helped me get him out to the parking lot. Even though it was night, the parking lot was well lighted, so we drew a lot of attention. When we got back to the T-Bird, we discovered that someone had stolen the front bucket seat on the driver's side!

I became somewhat anxious and told Ben we would have to leave the car and take a cab home.

Ben suddenly became calm and said, "Get a goddamn box or barrel to sit on and you'll be able to drive it." Which is what we did.

Ben had a major impact on my life both emotionally and financially. I like to believe that the nurturing and care I brought to him were responsible for the progress he made in life. After eight years of treatment, Ben was able to live in a home on the beach with a married couple (both nurses) and his faithful cook and housekeeper and, at last report, was doing reasonably well.

About this time it became increasingly apparent that it was time for my family and me to leave LA. I felt I was wasting my life there.

I never had contact with Ben again after we left. The good-bye was very difficult for both of us, and I felt that further communication would have been too hard on Ben. It was now time for him to swim without his lifeguard.

Chapter 8

It's impossible to spend ten years practicing psychiatry in a place like Hollywood without collecting a multitude of interesting case histories. In this land of fairy tales and narcissism, rare and wonderful stories abound.

The Knothole at Hollywood Park

Sam, an actor in his late twenties, came to see me for his depression. He had made a career out of being an actor but had not been as successful as he wished to be, in spite of doing several movies and TV shows. He was afraid people would find out about his being "gay." He had a compulsion to "cruise" on Friday and Saturday nights and would pick up men on Mulholland Drive, overlooking the city, even knowing it was patrolled because it was a gay pickup area. He also went to Hollywood Park, also well known in this regard. In Hollywood Park he would enter one of the men's toilets and stick his penis through a hole, as was the custom, and some stranger would perform fellatio on him, or vice versa. He acknowledged this was very exciting to him, that he could not resist, but he was also fearful that undercover LAPD officers would catch him and he'd make the papers and his career would be over.

Sam, a good actor and very handsome, was seen frequently in the company of very pretty women, and he told me he had "finger-fucked" several renowned and beautiful actresses.

Sam stayed in therapy with me for four years during which time he also "fell in love with me" as part of the positive transference. We interpreted the meanings involved but, of course, never touched. Progress was made in that he accepted his homosexuality, stopped having risky sex, and got into a monogamous long-term relationship with another male that was kept from public view. He apparently found someone quite like me with whom he could establish emotional intimacy and was no longer driven by the loneliness that had led him into self-destructive behaviors. He made a movie in Hong Kong and brought me back a statue of "Fear Man" that I still have in my office. I see him in films now and doing commercials that have class!

The Jewish Rifle

While in LA, I was consulted by a Jewish pharmacist thirty years of age who owned a chain of pharmacies. He was distressed that he was about to act out some of his fantasies about sitting on a ridge overlooking the Hollywood Freeway and shooting at German-made cars. Distant relatives had been subject to severe pogroms, but LA is not in general a particularly anti-Semitic town and I was puzzled as to the origin of his impulses.

I noted that he had been married for five years and that he was working long hours supervising his pharmacies. He had two young sons, aged three and five, whom he adored and identified with. His wife was mainly interested in shopping and redecorating the house. She was also involved with the children's religious activities and running a kosher kitchen. Jacob talked fondly of his wife and children but described his mother-in-law as a *yenta* (malicious gossip).

I asked Jacob to free-associate on the topic of anger.

"Make your mind a complete blank and share all your thoughts as they come to mind, no matter what they might be," I told him.

Jacob agreed to cooperate. Shortly he began to laugh.

"Jewish jokes, that's all that comes to mind!" he said.

"Tell me the jokes," I replied.

"How do you stop a Jewish woman from having sex?"

"I don't know," I said.

"You marry her!"

"What's the other joke?" I queried after chuckling appreciatively.

"How can you tell when a Jewish woman is having an orgasm?"

Again I replied that I didn't know.

"She drops her knitting needle!"

He then said that affection, nurturing, and communication had diminished with his wife since their marriage, a problem that had gotten worse after the birth of their sons. He stated he would buy an hour of time weekly from prostitutes near Hollywood and Vine "just to talk and get me understanding."

I then asked if it could be that he was very angry with his wife, but had such guilt about it that he had repressed it. I suggested that the anger could only be released indirectly by the jokes he told. He could displace his anger on the Germans, who were persecutors, but not direct it at his wife, whom he loved. I also asked him what responsibility *he* had in the breakdown of their relationship. He indicated that he had been spending too many hours making a lot of money and neglecting his family. He vowed to correct this.

After another eight sessions, he stated that he and his wife were now getting along well and that he was also spending more time with his children. He no longer needed to or wanted to shoot at German cars. In fact, he stated that he was thinking of getting a Mercedes since he had earned it.

Some years later, after no contact, I received an invitation to come to his son's bar mitzvah and the party that followed. The band that played at the party in the hotel included Ziggy Elman, who played my request "And the Angels Sing," as he had on his trumpet with Benny Goodman. The evening was bittersweet because Ziggy said he was dying of liver disease, to which he succumbed not long afterward.

The Cucumber

Donnel was a thirty-five-year-old bachelor opera singer when he was referred to me for psychotherapy by an ER physician of a local hospital. Donnel had gone to the ER because he feared "something terrible was going to happen."

His symptoms when he came to my office were a sense of impending doom, fear of loss of control, fear that he would die, and fear that he would do something he "might regret." He also had rapid pounding of the heart, dry mouth, frequency of urination, diarrhea, a knot in his stomach, and cold, clammy hands with numbness and tingling.

His past history revealed that his father had committed suicide when Donnel was only three years old. As an only child he was raised by his mother, who was a member of the Jehovah's Witnesses. She apparently never remarried, nor did she ever date again. She spent all her energies on her son, devoting herself to raising him. Donnel perceived his mother as a controlling, dominating, intrusive, and judgmental person, but it took four months of telling his life story, an hour a week, before he could bring himself to make such brave statements.

After eight months of work, he spontaneously told me, "I think she is unknowingly making me take the place of her husband. I don't think she likes men either. Dad, she says, was a 'wimp' and when he drank, he would beat her." Donnel added, "She says she loves me, but I can't figure out if the way she treats me is out of love or hate. I can't stand it when she goes to the bathroom and leaves the door open or walks in front of me in her underwear."

Donnel indicated that he had always done well with his studies. He graduated in the upper one-third of his high school class, excelling in music and shunning athletics. He was felt to be a "sissy" by his peer group and was teased incessantly. He retreated into a world of art and music and daydreamed a great deal. Always well-mannered and well-behaved, he never got angry and never cried and his only sexual activity consisted of wet dreams. He told me that he was worried that he might be gay but never had shared this with anyone before. He said he would rather be dead than queer. He had graduated from a small religious college, majoring in voice and music. He was a tenor.

Donnel developed a strong attachment to me, seeing me as an appropriate male role model. I helped him to express his feelings, to be angry when appropriate, to cry, to be assertive, and even to masturbate when he was alone. When I asked him what his fantasies were during this activity, he turned crimson. I asked him if the fantasies were about his mother. He shook his head no.

"About me?" I asked.

He sheepishly nodded yes.

"I'm glad you can share your fantasies," I replied, getting more relaxed in my chair. He grinned slightly and also began to relax.

Two years later he informed his mother that he was moving out and into his own apartment. She was shattered and threatened suicide. Donnel called her minister, who came to her aid, but he did move out. Donnel's career as an operatic tenor became increasingly successful, and he became rather well-known. He would stop by for a session whenever he came to town "for support." He informed me that he was happy with his career and his music but confessed one last thing to me before he terminated treatment. He felt that in order to hit the "high notes" he had to insert a cucumber up his rectum before singing. I asked him if he wished to talk about this further.

"No," he stated and I respected his wishes.

I would occasionally see him fondling the cucumbers in the vegetable section at the supermarket on Sunday mornings but always pretended I didn't see him. I seldom eat a cucumber even now without thinking of him.

The Owl

One of my patients, whose father owned a national restaurant chain, came in to see me about life issues complicated by anxiety and depression. She was twenty-three years old, had a six-year-old son, and worked in her father's business as a manager. She saw me weekly for about a year and a half and "got well."

I received a package at the office one day and found an owl inside, dressed like Sigmund Freud. I pulled the string and the owl spoke in a Viennese accent. The length one pulled the string would determine the phrase the owl would speak, i.e., "Lie down on the couch"; "I don't know; what do you think?"; "Why do you hate your mother?"; and "That will be $100!"

I usually don't accept gifts from patients unless they are psychotic. I do keep those, because to reject them would be too traumatic for these people. I decided, however, to keep Sigmund the Owl because I enjoyed him so!

Some months later during one session of a therapy group that had been together for about six months and was working well on their problems, they stopped interacting with each other and began asking me questions, something I generally discourage. As the questions continued, after my calling their attention to this, I went to get Sigmund the Owl and kept pulling the string after each question to me.

"I don't know; what do you think?" Sigmund would say.

This continued for twenty to thirty minutes, and the group members became extremely angry with me and berated me for not answering their questions. They expressed rage at Sigmund and the same time told me all the traits about me they disliked. It was the latter that was interfering with their treatment, they said, which led to the questioning me. After venting their anger at me, to which I said, "I'm delighted that you can tell me how you feel," the group began to interact with each other in a healthy way again.

The Attack of the Frozen Zucchini

Bill and Alice came to me for conjoint marital therapy. Alice had consulted me first, saying that Bill came from a dysfunctional family and that his mother slept around with other men and beat him severely when he was young. Alice also stated that her husband had difficulty accepting any kind of tenderness, had a violent temper, and preferred to get involved in sports activities with his buddies, after which he and his friends would go drinking at bars.

Although they had been married seven years, she reported that what finally brought her in to see me was that whenever he made love to her, he would make cricketlike noises while fingering and licking her belly button. She stated that this annoyed her so much that she attempted to avoid having sex with him or would just be passive, which infuriated him. When he would become angry with her, he would frequently attack her vaginally with a frozen zucchini, which he kept ready in the refrigerator.

After two sessions with them that went nowhere, I decided I would have to see Bill alone to attempt to resolve his anger toward women and to gain insight into how he was venting rage on his wife, by debasing and humiliating her, rather than taking it out on his mother.

In his first session alone with me Bill stated, "What are all those fools doing on *my freeway,* slowing me down when I'm trying to be here on time!"

After about fifteen sessions with me, he decided to terminate the relationship. The improvements he showed were: (1.) He now said, "Why are these fools driving in my *lane* [on the freeway]?" (2.) he stopped making cricketlike noises 90 percent of the time when having intercourse with his wife; and (3.) he no longer attacked his wife with a frozen zucchini. The nonfrozen one was, however, used about six times a year!

The Minister

This forty-two-year-old minister of a large, Protestant church was happily married and had a son and a daughter in college. He had no prior episodes of illness. His only complaint was that he was overworked and being "sucked dry" by the emotional needs of his congregation.

Raymond came to me for treatment of depression: he had crying spells, found it hard to concentrate, had lost his appetite, and had lost twenty pounds. He would awaken at 4:00 A.M. and find it impossible to get back to sleep. He lost interest in things he used to enjoy and had fleeting suicidal thoughts, consisting of fantasies of running his car into a bridge or tree at a high speed.

The precipitating event in this instance was the death of the president of the church board of trustees. This man was twenty years the minister's senior and had been counseled by him for two years for serious depression. The man refused to see a physician and felt psychiatrists were "crazy." (Ann Landers has said that

"Only 50 percent of psychiatrists are competent.") After spending a great deal of time with his friend, including night calls and weekends, Raymond found the man hanging in the barn on his farm. The minister felt a deep sadness, which brought him to see me.

I entered him into one of my therapy groups, with seven other patients who were well educated and successful. He came for the two-hour sessions weekly while I monitored the suicidal risk factors. He rarely participated in the group verbally but was most attentive to what the other patients said. At about the tenth group session, he jumped up and screamed, "That fucking cocksucker, son of a bitch bastard mother-fucker!" The group initially was shocked by the intensity of his verbal productions but then became more supportive. A doctor in the group said, "Tell us more about it." The minister shared in great detail the closeness he had with his friend and all the support he had given him.

He stated, "The bastard didn't even have the decency and trust to call me after all I did to help him. I could have saved him. I hate the son of a bitch. I'm glad he's dead. I'd like to kick his tombstone!"

The lawyer in the group said, "I respect you for sharing that with us. Do you want company when you kick the tombstone?" The group then volunteered to go to the cemetery with the minister and watched him while he cursed out his friend and actually kicked the tombstone!

The next week the group members asked if they could join the minister's church or at least come whenever they could to hear his sermons. A month later the minister's depression cleared and he stated that he was ready to leave the group.

A month after that I received a letter from him signed: "Love, Raymond." He thanked me for my help. He also stated that he had told his congregation that since he worked on his sermons on Saturdays, he would be taking Mondays off. He also stated that the congregation could no longer "drop in" to see him without an appointment and that evenings were reserved for his family unless there was an "extreme emergency." His congregation apparently understood and even had more respect for him than before.

The minister told me this was the first time he had ever "cussed and taken the Lord's name in vain." I surmised he would never do so again. I wrote him a note and told him I had the greatest respect for him as a person and as a minister.

Carol and the Closet Queens

Carol gave her history in her first appointment with me. Mark and Moe were grade-school friends; they had attended high school together and both had lettered in baseball, basketball, and swimming. They were together constantly and they frequently dated together as they grew older. Both were quite handsome, but their various masculine pursuits, playing ball, watching most of the games on TV, hunting and fishing and camping, drag racing, and golf, kept them busy enough to have infrequent dates. Moe got one girlfriend pregnant and "had to" get married.

Following his marriage, Moe began to spend even more time with Mark, who married two years later and purchased a home almost next to the one occupied by Moe and his wife. Moe became an accountant, and Mark went into sales, necessitating frequent traveling. Both men professed resentment and fear of "queers." In fact, Bill had been approached by one in a movie theater bathroom and had "decked him and stomped him."

Both were handsome and attracted a lot of attention. They got perms and frequently wore frilly shirts and quality cologne when dressing up. Carol described the two friends as enjoying each other more than their wives, avoiding emotional intimacy, being threatened by assertive behavior on the part of their wives and more concerned about their own orgasms than their wives'. Both women felt that their husbands might not be capable of a commitment to them, and so they were hesitant to get pregnant.

The description of the husbands is in keeping with the concept of the "phallic man" so frequently seen in our culture, macho yet brittle, not capable of commitment or tenderness, fucking with anger instead of making love.

Following a long argument with her husband, Carol felt extremely angry. Her husband's leaving on a business trip aggravated the matter. As she was left unsatisfied by a "quickie" with Mark before he left, her rage increased. Mark's oft-repeated comment that she'd better not fool around with other men while he was gone just added fuel to the fire. Always accused but never guilty, she got revenge on her husband by seducing Moe when he came over looking for Mark thirty minutes after he had left.

After she finished sharing this information with me, I asked her if she felt Mark saw her as being a "support system for a vagina in which he could masturbate."

Carol indicated that was exactly how she felt. When she told me about the sexual contact with Mark and then with Moe a half hour later, I told her that probably Mark's sperm were now kissing Moe's sperm in her vagina, saying, "I love you," to each other. Carol left the room retching but returned in a short time after vomiting in the ladies' room.

Six months later Carol divorced Mark because he refused to come to marriage counseling and did not accede to her requests to improve the marriage. Mark never knew of her hostile seduction of his buddy Moe, which is surprising, considering that divorce often leaves people a way to punish their ex-spouse.

The Squeeze

In the mideighties I treated an All-Pro linebacker from an East Coast team for substance abuse. He had been free-basing cocaine after games and when under emotional stress. He entered the hospital under the alias "Joe Smith," which was ludicrous because everyone recognized him. Besides that, while he was in residence there, his coach came down to work out with him on the hospital grounds.

He talked to me about being raised in the Deep South in poverty by his parents, who had many children. He had developed a religious value system, since his father was a Lutheran minister. Sudden fame and immense wealth had changed his life, and he found it difficult to cope. Women he had never met obtained his home phone number and called him for sex and money. In addition, his wife was pregnant and nonnurturing to him at the time because she also found it difficult to cope with their new lifestyle.

He told me about free-basing coke, "Take the best orgasm you've ever had in your whole life and multiply it by 1 million and you've got what that devil can do for you."

He talked about parties after games where players would have group sex with women who came for the coke; at times they would debase the women by doing kinky things such as urinating on them. I found it difficult to accept that these things were true. Perhaps he was "putting me on."

We worked together daily for several weeks, and he gained insight into some of his actions. I learned of his gratitude by the way he said good-bye. He gave me a hug that almost fractured my ribs. It has been my experience that addiction to free-basing cocaine is almost impossible to give up, which may have been true with him, since he retired prematurely from football a few years later.

Scarface

Claude was a forty-five-year-old retired navy veteran who had developed a belief that his face was "misshapen and ugly." It started when he was stationed on the island of Guam. He had seen various physicians, plastic surgeons, and was told there was nothing wrong with his face. These consultations did not change his belief that he was ugly.

He isolated himself from everyone, except his wife, and led a reclusive existence in his castle/fortress (his home) for many years. I made the diagnosis of body dysmorphic disorder and treated him with two milligrams of haloperidol at bedtime. When I saw him again six weeks later, he was smiling and happy and relieved that his face was now "normal." He had begun to socialize and go out to have a "great time." He believed it to be a miracle that a drug could heal his face so well. No attempt was made to give him psychological insight into the dynamics. All those wasted years were a real tragedy, since the diagnosis and the treatment were so simple.

Femme Fatale

I had been seeing this attractive model from North Hollywood for six months, one hour weekly. She was unhappily married and had a narcissistic personality disorder. The previous week I had made a particularly painful interpretation to her about her being rejected by her father. Her husband was very handsome but immature and could not live up to the idealized image she had of him. I suggested that perhaps she might be be very angry with all men. She left the session without comment, seemingly confused.

She returned the following week immaculately dressed in a micro-mini skirt, looking very beautiful. She sat seductively on the couch while I waited for her first comments. Instead she stood up and slowly began to undress.

"What are you doing?" I asked.

"What do you think I'm doing, Doctor?"

I didn't comment.

She stood there nude before me and said, "I want you to love me!"

"Are you angry with me about the interpretation I made last week about your father?" I said as calmly as I could. She was very beautiful.

She ignored my question. "Come on; if you're a man, you'll fuck me!"

"I don't think that would be in your best interest," I said. "Your therapy is my concern. It's a lot easier to find someone to fuck you than it is to find a competent psychiatrist!"

Angrily she got back into her clothes and left without a word.

A week later she came back to see me.

"Guess what I've done since last week?" she said. "I picked up and fucked ten different men and it's all your fault. You must be a goddamned queer. No one's ever turned *me* down before, and I hate you!"

Gently I said, "Perhaps now we can continue our discussion about your father. I'd like to help you."

Sheepishly she said, "OK."

"In the future, particularly when we have a painful session, could you put your feelings into words and tell me about them rather than acting them out?"

"I'll try . . . "

That was the beginning of her recovery.

Victor/Victoria

A young woman came to see me who was demurely dressed, as one might expect of a person from the historic part of Williamsburg, Virginia. I learned that she was really a young man who was a transsexual who wished to go to Johns Hopkins University Hospital for sex-change surgery. Therapy was mandatory before being considered for such surgery. This young man was motivated to have the surgery but seemingly not motivated for the therapy.

We agreed to begin our discussion by having a one-hour session each week. He was usually on time and shared some of his current life experiences with me. On one occasion, he had gone cruising to a local bar and was "picked up" by an alleged osteopathic physician who took him to a local hotel. They kissed and fondled, but the DO then apparently demanded intercourse even though my patient had stated, "I'm on the rag." The physician became enraged when he found out his "pickup" had a penis. He attempted to thrash my patient, who escaped but was chased down the street by the irate physician.

As my patient learned that I was truly interested in helping him, the manner in which he related to me changed markedly. His dresses began to get shorter and shorter, and he would sit seductively exposing his panties (with the penis bulge). I called his attention to this, wondering what the possible motivation might be.

He stated, "I guess I'm falling in love with you and want to see if I can turn you on."

I said, "Perhaps you're showing me that you still have a penis, which might indicate that your mother didn't get to you [i.e., take away the penis by castration]!"

As therapy continued Victor/Victoria became rather confused

about whether he wished to go through with the surgical procedure or not. He became very depressed and made a suicidal gesture by ingesting his mother's tranquilizers, so I admitted him to the psychiatric ward of a local hospital for observation. The reasons for the attempt were unclear at the time, but it appeared that he feared the therapy more than having the surgery.

I had another patient in the hospital at the same time. He was a sixty-three-year-old Jewish internist who had a coronary after his wife died about five years before. He attempted to be quite a ladies' man thereafter but was depressed because he felt he would soon be dead. He became serious about his suicidal intentions after he was rejected by a young woman he had attempted to date.

Victor/Victoria looked absolutely "gorgeous" in the patients' lounge in the hospital. Dr. Abe came up to him and began to flirt with him, snuggling up to steal a kiss. Suddenly Victor/Victoria pulled off his wig, shocking the internist severely. Other people felt he was going to have another coronary.

Victor/Victoria left the hospital shortly thereafter. Two weeks later he had his mother call me to say that her son had left town and to assure me that he was OK. I did not hear from him for six months, when he called to request a letter saying that he had completed therapy for the Johns Hopkins University sex-change operation. I refused to write the letter, as he had just begun the therapy and had at least two to five years' worth to complete. I never heard from him again.

Practicing psychiatry in Woodland Hills was bittersweet. It was interesting to treat the "rich and famous," but as I had been a great movie fan all of my life and idealized the stars, there were a great many disappointments. During those years of giving care to these people, I came to a number of conclusions about some of them:

1. Many of the greatest male lovers on the screen were gay.
2. Many of the femmes fatales in movies changed clothes in the bathroom so their husbands/lovers couldn't see their nude bodies.

3. Writers of wonderful love songs hadn't been in their wives' bedrooms for years.
4. Actors who played nurturing and caring father figures on the screen could be very abusive to their children.
5. A jazz singer I adored when growing up was strung out on heroin.
6. Some people needed support in groups for years and years without getting better, but it did help them survive and prevented their conditions from worsening.
7. Stars are likely to have personality disorders (mixed, narcissistic, histrionic), which are persistent, with consistent styles of behavior that frequently are associated with emotional immaturity.
8. Many of them come from dysfunctional families. For them applause equals love, the need of which for them is insatiable.
9. They feel "entitled" and are "needy": "I need to see you immediately, Doctor!"
10. They need you desperately when they lose a TV series, but the need for therapy diminishes when they get another one and they frequently terminate care then.
11. They do not handle feelings well. Emotional intimacy and anger can be threatening when felt toward the psychiatrist. They often feel hostile when the doctor makes an in-depth interpretation about their problems. They frequently escape by "going on location."
12. As a general rule, the bigger the star, the slower the payment for my services.
13. If they like you, they will refer their friends and colleagues to you.

Chance Encounters I Had While Traveling at the Time I Was Living in LA

My wife and I had been shopping in Harrods department store in London. As we exited into the street, in a downpour, I bumped into Peter Ustinov. I said, "Peter, is it really you?" He smiled and we exchanged pleasantries.

Flying out of LA to Mexico, we noted that Ursula Andress was sitting directly in back of us with Jean-Paul Belmondo and across the aisle were George Kennedy and Ben Wright. I chose not to intrude on their privacy.

While staying on the third deck of the Peninsula Hotel in Hong Kong, I met Cliff Robertson, who had just won an Oscar for his movie *Charley.* I congratulated him and he thanked me.

While leaving the Hotel Österreicher in Vienna (where Julie Andrews stayed during the filming of *The Sound of Music*) I saw David Niven at the bar. I said, "Greetings from Los Angeles, David." He came over and chatted with us for forty minutes or so. He was making a movie, *When Winter Comes.* He was cordial and gracious, as though we had always been friends.

Chapter 9

In June of 1971, Rosemarie and I decided it was time to leave LA. There were numerous very compelling reasons for wanting to go. First of all, we were perched on the notorious San Andreas fault line. We had already survived an earthquake that registered 6.5 on the Richter scale and scared the hell out of us! There was no desire to repeat the experience.

Equally as offensive was the smog, which was getting worse by the month, it seemed. Porno theaters and strip bars were moving closer to our neighborhood near Ventura Boulevard, in addition to the drugs and drug dealers who came to the affluent areas and preyed upon everyone's children.

Our neighborhood itself was no longer a safe, comfortable place to live. Many of the houses in the area had been burglarized. Several unruly neighbors were constantly drag-racing on the street, holding late night parties, cutting down my cactus garden, and throwing oranges at us in the pool. Some of the rowdies causing us such discontent included a famous movie star's grown children. We called the police numerous times, since we were the only ones on the block who weren't afraid to do so. We arranged a meeting with most of the people on the block and the county attorney to discuss the situation. Unfortunately, all our efforts were in vain.

Also, I had grown tired of the self-centered, narcissistic class of patients that I was taking care of. The last straw came when I received a call at 2:00 A.M. from an actress saying she needed to see me at once or she would kill herself, because she had gotten notice that she was getting second billing in an upcoming movie.

Rosemarie and I put our house up for sale, but every time someone came to look at the place the rowdies would drag-race, curse, and threaten the prospective buyers. Eventually we sold the house, but for $20,000 dollars less than we paid for it. Two years after we left, the real estate in Los Angeles went out of sight! Our house would have been worth $250,000 by then instead of the $65,000 we had received.

I flew around the country looking for a place that would provide good employment and a safe environment for raising our family. I found just what we were looking for in Traverse City, Michigan, on Grand Traverse Bay, with access to Lake Michigan.

We arrived in Traverse City and were given a large home on the beautiful Traverse City State Hospital grounds, which were covered with wooded areas of maple and pine, a salmon-filled stream wandering through the grounds. The architecture of the various buildings on the hospital grounds was one of contrast, with many old historical buildings intermingled with a new administration building and receiving unit.

We loved the beauty of the area, particularly Old Mission Peninsula, and the small-town atmosphere. We purchased a home nestled in the corner of a cherry orchard, overlooking Grand Traverse Bay. The two older children were initially very unhappy about leaving their friends in LA but gradually adjusted to their new home.

I was the Director of the Receiving Hospital and shortly after arrival was appointed Assistant Clinical Professor, Department of Psychiatry, College of Human Medicine, Michigan State University. Due to the sudden illness of the assistant superintendent, I was made clinical director and in essence was responsible for running the clinical components of the hospital There was a residency program in psychiatry already in place, as well as a teaching clerkship for medical students supported by visiting faculty from MSU and clinical faculty in residence. Many of the resident physicians had graduated from foreign medical schools and had language and cultural problems.

As clinical director my first goal was to do away with the dehumanizing practices currently in existence in the hospital. Just before our move from LA, *Time* magazine had a paragraph about one of our patients who had allegedly been beaten to death by ward attendants. A lawsuit was pending, and follow-up autopsies had been performed.

The hospital superintendent, a kind and knowledgeable man,

had been under attack by a local newspaper ever since he withdrew advertising from the local newspaper and used his contacts in town to encourage others to do the same. The paper folded and the superintendent was sued for his alleged responsibility for the paper's demise. The controversy that ensued allowed a dissident group at the hospital, composed primarily of the people in the residency teaching program and the chief neurologist, to attempt to get him removed. I cast my lot with the superintendent, who was replaced not too long thereafter. He moved to a retirement community in Arizona. After his wife's death, he was pursued by numerous widows.

My next step was to ensure that the psychopharmacology treatment was being done appropriately, that is, no more polypharmacy. Many of the staff psychiatrists were marginally qualified, so instead I worked largely with the nurses, psychologists, and social workers to improve the clinical programs. They said they had been waiting for someone like me to come along.

We started group therapy on all the wards and allowed the patients to listen in on the subsequent postgroup staff discussions. We also started patient government meetings, reduced seclusion by 90 percent by limiting it to a strict criterion such as a danger to others and not for such simple misdemeanors like saying, "shit."

I followed the Milton Greenblatt, M.D., method of not requiring a consensus but instead getting power and using it directly. It is more painful this way, because others like their input to be considered and to be "democratic" in proceeding. The other way, however, has proven highly effective and was not so time-consuming. We provided evening therapy so that patients would not be put to bed early just so that staff could enjoy themselves. I also toured the underground tunnels to see what was happening at odd hours. At times patients were discovered making love. Sometimes it was the staff. I found the wild cats interesting, as they largely controlled the tunnels at night.

We asked that patients be addressed as Mr., Miss, or Mrs. to show them respect. These changes led to a good deal of hostility by the authoritarian, controlling group that had worked in the hospital for years, generation after generation. I opened my office door one morning and found all my diplomas piled high on my desk surrounded by horse manure and a cryptic note that said: "From the Staff." This seemed to be in response to my vetoing hours of chair sitting for three young children who had escaped from the children's unit and terminating what would have been three days in seclusion for them. I did not feel particularly annoyed by these actions, but the new superintendent was appalled by the infantile actions of some of the staff in the children's unit.

Despite the stress of my work, the whole family was enjoying Traverse City. We got a sailboat, canoe, Alpine and cross-country skis, and a new German shepherd to replace our older one, who had developed breast cancer just before we left LA and had to be put to sleep. There were vast areas to walk, morel mushrooms to be discovered in the spring, and salmon to be caught in the stream that traversed the hospital grounds.

I became friends with the owners of the Cherry County Playhouse and met all the stars who played there and was able to attend the postperformance parties for the stars at the owner's home at Northport Point. Pat Paulsen later bought the playhouse and affectionately called me Hamburger, because that was his favorite phrase for intimate friends. I brought Goober, my friend and neighbor from LA, to Traverse City to be grand marshal of the Cherry Parade and star at the Cherry County Playhouse. During a stunt in the play, he aggravated an old knee injury he had gotten from playing football for the University of Alabama. While he was thus hobbled, I took him to the chronic ward at the hospital and introduced him to the patients. They all recognized him and asked for his autograph and to touch him. This strangeness and cloying attention frightened him, and he said, "Get me the hell out of here, Walter!"

The Traverse City State Hospital had up to fifteen hundred patients in residence at any one time in the years leading up to 1971. State of Michigan budget crunches, however, required the hospital to reduce the census to about five hundred inhabitants through a process of deinstitutionalizing the least dangerous of our patients. Many of these troubled and psychotic people were discharged and remained in the Traverse City area. Their presence led to numerous social problems and an increased feeling of resentment in the area toward the hospital, especially since no one in the community had been allowed any input in the process.

The hospital had very few board-certified psychiatrists, and many of its physicians could not communicate effectively in English or understand the culture. The staffing did, however, at least enable us to meet the patients' basic needs, even if it didn't allow for effective psychiatric treatment. Unfortunately, there was more a desire to control patients with medications rather than utilizing communication and understanding. Drugs were expedient. Actually, getting to know the patients was apparently too much effort.

After the initial period of learning how the place ran and then evaluating the hospital's shortcomings, I was able to institute changes by early 1972. I had support from the superintendent and about ten of the physicians, 80 percent of the social workers and psychologists, and about 50 percent of the nurses, the more junior ones. There was a strong resistance from the "old guard," but we did not allow it to deter us from making the required changes.

We arranged for my staff and me to have coffee with the patients on all of the wards, regular meetings with staff on all three shifts at their workplace, and periodic discussions with the janitors, cooks, and security people to enlist their support as well.

The changes we created made so much sense and were so successful that it still surprises me that we met so much resistance. Apparently, change itself is traumatic even under normal circumstances, let alone when handling emotionally disturbed patients. Most of the improvements were based on techniques that had been proven to be successful in other hospitals.

Half the hospital wards were made into open units after careful screening of patients was done. Patients who would not fit into this format were transferred to other floors. Open units allowed for more "normalization" with more freedom, which in turn emphasized personal responsibility and normal consequences. Doctors' offices were placed on the wards to facilitate access to patients and staff and to develop therapeutic alliances with them.

Polypharmacy was abolished for the most part. Individual cases of polypharmacy that continued had to be justified by documentation and peer review. The staff learned that antipsychotic drugs all acted in basically the same way except for their side effects, which could be either a help or a hindrance. The staff also observed that less medication is often "more" in terms of benefit and that untoward interactions of various drugs at times made patients much worse.

Seclusion was reduced by 90 percent by making dangerous acts the only justification for the initiation of the procedure. Seclusion was solitary confinement with only a mat in the room. Each ward had to graph weekly seclusion hours, and a 10 percent reduction was expected each week. Consultation was provided to wards that did not comply. I began to hold weekly staffings of the few difficult patients who accounted for the majority of the seclusion hours. Many of these patients required more intensive treatment but sometimes less. The staff was taught new and more effective methods of coping with the patients' disturbing behavior. As a consequence the staff began to feel more competent in their professional roles and became more interested in understanding patients' actions, thereby becoming more therapeutic in their interaction with patients instead of being afraid of them.

Modified "therapeutic community" meetings were started on all wards. These allowed patients to express their thoughts and feelings to the staff, and vice versa. They also provided education and emotional growth for all the participants. In addition, they made patients more responsible for their own behavior, with peer group feedback and monitoring to help the process. The staff began to see patients as having the same needs and fears as themselves. As a result we started to see the employees treat the patients as they would like to have their own family members cared for.

However, dehumanizing practices such as excessive seclusion, treating patients as children, not allowing them to hold hands or, if in a relationship, kiss, putting them to bed early, referring to them by diagnosis rather than name, and making fun or threatening them were not sanctioned and were dealt with by calling continuous attention to these situations and stressing each person's uniqueness as a human being and the roles they had played in life before becoming ill. As a result of our efforts, empathy replaced sympathy.

We also stressed continuously that the lack of love in the patients' lives could be partially compensated for by our showing them respect. We believed that their anxieties might respond better to communication rather than to psychotropics alone. It seemed to us that their guilt feelings might be ameliorated by giving them understanding rather than frequent admonitions and demands for "positive thinking." We made it a policy that "it is considered malpractice to give medications without giving love at the same time."

After implementing many of these changes, which included modernization of treatment programs, staff education, and decentralization, we petitioned the superintendent to allow me to develop a division of community mental health for the benefit of our discharged patients who continued to cause serious community problems. These ex-patients were frequently unable to take care of their own basic needs and were often exploited by "predators" who wanted their money and often their bodies. The chamber of commerce and community leaders were concerned about the city's reputation as a tourist mecca being compromised by homeless psychotic patients living in rooming houses or cheap hotels downtown. The local Act 54 Board had just begun to organize but was still two to three years away from beginning to function in terms of delivery services.

After no response from the superintendent for several months, we finally obtained permission to explore the concepts we had proposed with local agencies, which gave strong support to this program. In August of 1973 we were informed that the Division of Community Mental Health could become a reality.

The superintendent set September 28, 1973, as the day for the reorganization, utilizing a "pro-football draft" to choose professional staff for the two new divisions, which were based on geography. It began with a coin flip between a service chief and the director of clinical programs (me). The Division of Community Mental Health, with fifty current inpatients, was to be responsible for the county in which the hospital was located and the four contiguous counties. The Distal Division was to take responsibility for the other twenty-eight counties and approximately three hundred inpatients. The professional staff was to be divided equally between the two. The two divisions were informally called "the Mod Squad," based on a then-popular TV series, and the "North Woods Conglomerates."

The community mental health unit took over the third floor of the Receiving Hospital and the outpatient clinic as its physical base of operation. Unfortunately, the manner in which the reorganization took place led to significant staff confusion, turmoil, and some bitterness. There was also a great deal of elation among those staff who had wished to join the advances already being made in hospitals in other areas of the country.

The Division of Community Mental Health entered the community gradually. We made contact with local clergy by giving lectures and seminars suited to their needs. After establishing rapport, we made them part of our treatment team when their parishioners were involved and helped them counsel difficult clients with emergencies in their own offices. Our senior staff was available to them day and night for telephone consultations. Many of the clergy commented that the invisible wall separating the state hospital from the city had been torn down at last.

The chief of police was pleased that I visited him in his office, saying that this was the first time anyone from the hospital had done so. We then exchanged cigars, and lit up and the rapport was further established. He said we could start by having me ride on all three shifts in the patrol cars with his officers to get to know them and the city's problem areas better. This was followed by approval for staff and medical students to do so as well. Because of our efforts, a very close and mutually supportive relationship developed that benefited everyone, particularly our discharged psychotic patients.

We gained access to the local drug crisis center, located in the center of the city in a storefront. This was run by former addicts and street people. We volunteered first-aid assistance at their rock concerts, which were also attended by "bikers" from Detroit and other areas. We also provided consultation and assistance with their hot-line volunteers, helping them to deal with suicidal clients and sadistic callers. As we established trust with them further, we volunteered evenings at the storefront to counsel their clients, who wished to remain anonymous. Later we staffed a clinic along with volunteers from other medical specialties from the local medical center. In addition, we helped to "mend fences" between the former substance abusers and the city police by having a Christmas party to which all were invited.

The sheriff's department was a problem area for us initially, as the sheriff had lost faith in state hospital psychiatrists from experiences with them in the past. When we developed a ten-bed crisis unit, furnished like a home and well staffed, by good fortune one of the first patients was a friend of the sheriff's. This led to acceptance of the division and helped us gain access to the jail, where we set up counseling services and furnished it with hospital furniture from closed hospital wards. Our relationship with the sheriff's department gradually became almost as close as it was with the city police. After a period of time, with the development of trust, I was invited to attend the bimonthly law enforcement breakfasts as a regular member. During these sessions, community problems were discussed by the district court judge, sheriff, police chief, Michigan State Police Commander, and myself.

The probate court expressed an interest in having our group do precommitment screenings for it. The probate judge would advise us when he had a petition for involuntary admission, and we would make a home visit on his behalf and advise him as to the validity of the petition and/or initiate treatment when this was feasible. We sent our most experienced staff on these calls, with the director taking his turn in rotation as well. We were able to cut admissions to the state hospitals by 70 percent, and I was asked to talk to a state conference of probate judges to explain our initiatives. In turn, the judge began to hold court at the hospital, allowing the family to bring the patient there rather than to the courthouse.

Each social agency in town had one of our staff members assigned to it for liaison consultation and support. Regular meetings were established to service patients who would otherwise "fall through the cracks."

Satellite clinics were set up in each of the contiguous counties and a treatment team (psychiatrist, psychologist, social worker, nurse, and medical student) would visit each county at least monthly, so that people would not have to miss work or children miss school to come to the outpatient clinic to see us. This tactic also offered an opportunity to get to know the caretakers of those counties. The same team would handle all the inpatient treatment from a specific county should one of their outpatients require it.

Referrals to the outpatient section of the division began to increase dramatically because of our public education efforts. I became the gatekeeper. (The most experienced clinician performed this responsibility.) I would make an initial assessment and treatment plan and then assign the patient to a "primary therapist" who by virtue of training, experience, and temperament would be the most helpful. The primary therapist was responsible not only for the patient and his family, but for extended family and any significant others as well. The primary therapist could get all the consultation he deemed necessary but retained responsibility for that patient, including inpatient work. The primary therapist was on call twenty-four hours a day for his patient just as in a private practice model. In order to promote growth experiences for the staff, there were times when we made intentional "mismatches" so the staff member could improve skills in other areas. The inpatient staff also did their own outpatient follow-ups.

The staff developed a downtown drop-in center, known as the Friendship Center, for discharged patients along with a brochure and newsletter from there. The center allowed discharged patients to socialize and recreate. Our staff attended by invitation to provide lectures and to conduct small groups and set ongoing support discussions on topics of interest. Although local agencies and volunteers helped with time, donations, and program development, the patients were primarily responsible for these activities and the continuation of the program.

We did program evaluation by having patients fill out questionnaires and then sent them, anonymously, to another agency and other interested parties such as the Mental Health Association for review and feedback. Patient representatives from inpatient and outpatient sections attended administrative meetings regularly to express areas of concern and unhappiness and make recommendations regarding new avenues of pursuit. Staff would often walk the streets to make contact with isolated patients who did not avail themselves of our program.

There were a number of incidents that demonstrated how the division functioned in the community.

We received a call from the probate judge asking for evaluation of a sixty-eight-year-old man who had had several previous hospitalizations for schizophrenia. I drove to his residence and introduced myself appropriately and established rapport by doing a physical examination on him. I then listened with him to the record player and TV, which were "sending threatening messages" to him. He then allowed me to give him an injection of prolixin decanoate. The possible side effects were explained to him, as well as the probability that he would start to feel better in two to three days. His wife and his personal physician were then called to apprise them of the patient's situation, which was almost in remission. We then relinquished his care to his doctor after telling him of my willingness to be of service in the future as necessary.

Another time we received a call from the police department stating that a drunken Native American was creating a disturbance at a local hotel. One of our senior psychiatrists knocked on the Indian's door and introduced himself. The Indian was obviously intoxicated and was holding a fifth of bourbon when he opened the door for the psychiatrist, who happened to be Korean.

Our psychiatrist established rapport by saying, "That looks like good whiskey. Can I have a swig?"

The Indian gave the psychiatrist his bottle, and after taking a sip, he asked the man what was troubling him.

The man began to cry, saying that his employer, a woman, hated him and so he was going to quit his job. Our psychiatrist then suggested they go for a walk around town together. At the end of an hour the man had sobered up and the doctor said he had to return to the clinic, since his lunch hour was up. The man replied that he was going back to work to talk with the employer to resolve things and that he felt much better.

The owner of a local hotel called us at eleven o'clock one night saying he was evicting a former patient of ours immediately for nonpayment of rent. I went to the hotel to see the patient and found her in a catatonic state. I talked to her gently, telling her we had a nice private room on an open ward for her in the hospital, which she could leave as soon as we found a new place for her to live in town. I asked her if she would like to come to the hospital voluntarily for the night to sleep in a nice warm bed. She consented and we loaded her belongings in my car and took her to our crisis unit. The next morning, she was much improved and we found a placement for her that suited her situation better.

The division received a call at 1:00 A.M. on a cold winter night from the sheriff's department advising us that a woman had gone berserk ten miles out in the country and was throwing stones at neighbors' houses and threatening to kill her husband. When I arrived at the scene, I found a large gathering of people at the house, an ambulance, and two sheriff's patrol cars. We knocked on the door and introduced ourselves and were immediately greeted by a barrage of profanities and told to "get the hell away." I asked the officer if he could help me get into the house for a moment. He went inside and I could hear a woman through the door screaming at him, "Do you see any bruises on him? My brothers are going to get me the hell out of here tomorrow. Now get out of here!"

We asked the officer what he thought, and he said that he felt the situation presented no danger. We concurred with him and he cleared the area and we all left.

One of our psychiatrists was seeing a five-foot-tall woman in the clinic. She had five children and was being physically abused by her six-foot, four-inch, 150-pound husband. He had refused to come to the clinic, so the satellite team made a home visit. The man was astounded when the psychiatrist knocked on his door with a nurse, social worker, psychologist, and two medical students. After exploring briefly the reason for the visit, the Korean psychiatrist, my best friend, Seuk Soon Im, M.D., noticed a violin on the wall and asked the man if he played. He nodded and so they asked him to play a tune for them. The staff first began to hum along and then started to sing the words. Before long the man joined in and so did his wife. Because we had broken down the barrier of distrust we were able to sit down together and discuss the issues. The man said he would come to the clinic the following week with his wife. On the way out of the house, Seuk whispered in the man's ear that he had a black belt in karate, so he ought not to strike his wife again or he would have to deal with the consequences. The man kept his promise and later improved with treatment. We all knew, including the man, the "threat" was actually meant to further rapport, not intimidate him.

A priest from a local church called the division asking for assistance. One of his parishioners had asked for our help because her son was threatening suicide in the city jail and she wished to bail him out again, as she had always done on numerous other occasions. Evaluation revealed a charming and verbal man whose arms were covered with tattoos ("Mother" in a heart and "Death before Dishonor"), with no evidence of depression or psychosis. We called the priest and suggested to him to counsel his parishioner that she ought to let her son take normal consequences for his actions and that he was a low suicidal risk. The priest thanked us but called an hour later in distress. He said the woman had severely berated him and was also angry with us for our suggestions. We arranged to see her, allowed her to ventilate her anger, then explained to her in simple terms how her behavior was contributing to her son's problems. She began to cry, which was the beginning of her becoming a patient of ours. She asked to gain further insight into her own behavior so she could stop it. The priest was party to the counseling, which proved to be successful.

On another occasion the police called saying that they had an emergency. A man had barricaded himself in a house with a shotgun and was surrounded by the police. We learned that the man had a fairly good relationship with his brother, so we called him and asked for his help. When he arrived, he walked to the front door with us to talk to the barricaded man and ask him to put down his gun. Unknown to all of us, the police had gained entry to the back of the house and they disarmed him. We felt a sense of relief, but also of betrayal, but chose not to express that feeling at that time to the lieutenant in charge. An agreement was later reached to communicate better in the future in such situations so that our word and trust would not be compromised again.

During this time the TV show *Dallas* was creating a great deal of excitement in town. Everyone wanted to know who shot "J.R." I was asked to explain on TV why people hated him and felt sorry for him at the same time. I suggested that J.R. openly expressed human feelings we all harbor but usually are less open in showing them. We secretly enjoy the character's vileness while at the same time condemning him in order to make ourselves feel less guilty. Our "feeling sorry" for him may also be related to our unconscious identification with him. When asked who shot him, I guessed (tongue in cheek), "The psychiatrist, of course." This was an opportunity to give the public a chance to think more about human dynamics and proved to be quite educational. The article made the front page of the local paper, with pictures of the *Dallas* stars and myself.

Ever ready to nip success in the bud, the state of Michigan in all of its distant wisdom withdrew the funding for the division, and it was deactivated in July of 1975.

Prior to that time, though, the APA and the Michigan Psychiatric Society reviewed my work at Traverse City State Hospital. I was honored at the annual meeting in Los Angeles and was given a silver medal and made a Fellow in the APA for "making significant contributions to the field of psychiatry."

In 1975 I decided to go into private practice in Traverse City. Rosemarie, Garrett, Tiffanie, Cindy, and I left the large green house at Elmwood and 11th and moved to Old Mission Peninsula, to a large A-frame house, located in a cherry orchard, on a bluff overlooking Grand Traverse Bay. The setting was idyllic and the views spectacular. We had our own beach and we were all happy with our new home. My office was located across the street from Dill's Saloon, a Traverse City landmark, in "Old Town." My practice flourished and I traded in the Eldorado for a new red Mercedes 450 SL, a purchase that in retrospect, I know was signifying a coming midlife crisis.

As I had experienced in LA, there were a number of patients in my private practice in Michigan that were memorable for me.

The Tomboy

During this time I had a patient who had been raised by her father to be a "tomboy." She was an excellent shot and a proficient hunter, baseball player, swimmer, and boxer. She had a rather masculine build and closely cropped hair. She had a degree in social work but soon came into therapy because of a great deal of anger, idealizing people and then denigrating them without apparent cause. She also had an intolerance for being alone but had no close friends. Her therapy with several other therapists had not worked out, and she was referred to me by a colleague. Her diagnosis was borderline personality disorder, which manifested itself by anger, difficulty in being alone, idealizing people then denigrating them, and brief psychotic episodes.

After seeing her weekly for several months, I began to notice that whenever she appeared to feel emotionally close to me she tended to become inordinately angry. On one occasion in the office she jumped up with her fists clenched and appeared to be ready to leap over the round table between us to assault me. I got into a defensive karate stance to ward off her blows. Suddenly she began talking and acting like a four-year-old child who wanted her grandmother. I took her by the hand, walked her to my car, and drove her to Munson Medical Center, where I hospitalized her. After two weeks of inpatient care, she reverted back to her normal personality, but with complete amnesia for the other personality. A month or two later she showed another personality that appeared to be that of a mischievous, irresponsible teenager. This, too, led to hospitalization and the eventual disappearance of this personality as well, again with complete amnesia. Later there developed a fourth personality, that of an evil male growing a mustache and beard. "He" was into witchcraft and Satanism and wanted to do "evil things." This personality also remitted. Oversimplifying greatly, I pointed out to the patient that there were three other personalities and that they were all "her." I told her I intended to hold her personally responsible for all the other personalities' behavior.

She had always been very dependent upon both her parents, who were alcoholics. They left for Florida in the winter and sent her a box of sand as a "present." She became enraged and said she was going to kill not only her father, mother, and dog, but also my dog, my three children, and then my wife and me. She described my family perfectly, the times they came home from school, where our German shepherd was tied up, and where our house was located. Then my time with this patient was up, and so I terminated the session, full of uneasiness about her threats.

I closed the office the following day, drove to the University of Michigan in Ann Arbor, and went to see the chairman of the Department of Psychiatry, looking for assistance. He did not answer my questions but referred me to the university library to review the literature on this subject.

I learned that patients who threatened their psychiatrists this way frequently took their own lives by committing suicide due to the therapist rejecting them. Fortunately and coincidentally, at this same time the University of Michigan was having a seminar on violence conducted by a visiting professor from Northwestern. I asked him questions about my situation, and (to oversimplify) he told me to tell the patient that I would not allow her threats and that the therapy would be over if she ever threatened me again.

I also shared with her what I had learned in the library, about patients such as her killing themselves. She appeared suddenly relaxed and was no longer angry. We had several more sessions, and then she never returned. After the final one, she wrote me a note that appeared to me to be suggesting suicide. I tried to locate her but to no avail.

A year later I received a wedding picture of her and a very nice-looking groom. On the back of the picture was one comment: "Thank you." Two years later I received another picture, again without a return address, this time with a baby now in the picture. A year later another picture and a second child. I never heard from her again. I assume she is happily married and having a good life.

Ebony and Ivory

I had been treating a white woman who was in a physically abusive relationship with a black man who was intensely jealous of her without any apparent reason. He had been in a gang while he was growing up in Philadelphia and was a Vietnam veteran. She felt certain he would kill her someday. I asked her if she had ever considered terminating the relationship with him.

I didn't get a response at the time, and she went home and told him that I had suggested she terminate the relationship with him. Late that night I received a phone call via my answering service. This man told me he had found where I lived and was coming out to throw acid in my face. I spent the night anxiously watching for his arrival.

The next morning I went to see the chief of police, then the county sheriff, and told them about the incident. I thought I remembered the patient telling me that the man was working in road construction just outside the city. I went to the office as usual but had an appointment card made out saying: "CALL POLICE—EMERGENCY!" if he should try to break in. I would give the card to the patient I was seeing at the time, who, I hoped, would be "excused."

My son called me from East Lansing and said some black friends of his indicated that the threat was probably not serious, because violent people would just do the act without wasting the time on threatening comments. The police officials said they would do what they could. The next day they called saying they had dealt with the matter and that it "was over." Apparently the man was "asked" to leave town. The police didn't tell me specifically what had happened, and I decided it was prudent not to ask.

Late in 1980, I separated from Rosemarie, filed for divorce, and moved into my office. My children's love and support made the transition easier than I had feared. I had no regrets.

I contacted my lawyer and instructed him to divide the family assets down the middle to be fair to Rosemarie, since we had been married twenty-six years and it was my desire to not have any hostility between us.

In the weeks that followed, a friend taught me about sharing and expressing feelings when my sister, seven years my junior, was killed in an automobile accident. My sister and I had never been close. She always excelled at everything and was my father's obvious favorite. Samuel Zisowicz, my high school honors English teacher, threw me out of class several times for talking. My sister Frieda, by contrast, was his favorite, and he would often play his violin for her after class.

In 1980, prior to our separation, Rosemarie and I had scheduled a trip to Morocco and Kenya and planned to take my father and our younger daughter, Tiffanie, who was sixteen at the time. The trip had been prepaid, and rather than abandon the trip, we decided to go anyway. I would room with my father and Rosemarie with Tiffanie. Needless to say, it was a difficult trip emotionally for all of us.

We visited several cities in Morocco and enjoyed the sights. We saw several French Foreign Legion forts, which brought back to mind one of my favorite movies, *Beau Geste.* In Marrakesh we had a real scare. We entered a huge open-air market, covering perhaps one hundred acres or more. In the market were magicians, entertainers, snake charmers, and numerous stalls full of produce, meat, art goods, and so forth, but no police. Disastrously, we became separated from our native guide in all the hubbub.

A gang of tough-looking Arabs separated Tiffanie and me from my wife and father. I put my arm around Tiffanie, who is very attractive and blond and blue-eyed. The toughs offered to buy her from me for 20,000 sheep! They kept insisting I give Tiffanie to them. At the same time several of them kept going for my wallet while the others tried to pull Tiffanie away from me. I searched around desperately for help, but none was available.

The incident lasted about fifteen minutes and the nightmare ended when our native guide appeared and started shouting at them. Miraculously, some of them dispersed. As we entered the guide's car one tough made one last grab for my wallet and I broke his wrist with a downward karate block.

In early 1981 I signed up for an adventure in the Amazon jungle some forty to sixty miles from where several missionaries had been murdered several years before by Auca Indians. We went by motor-powered canoe up the Black River, a tributary of the Amazon in Ecuador, and then into the jungle with an Indian guide. There were few trails and we were warned not to leave them, as there were bushmaster snake nests in the area. The bushmaster is the most poisonous snake in the world. We had to cut our way through the jungle with machetes and swung from vines from tall trees in a pale imitation of Tarzan.

We spotted a huge anaconda over twenty feet long in the water not far away from where we were hiking. We got into a dugout canoe in a lagoon and caught piranhas using raw beef as bait. Our fishing over with, the Indian guide then said we could go swimming. I confronted him about the danger because we had just caught the piranha. The guide said as long as I wasn't bleeding anywhere it was OK to go in. I told him it was the "right time of the month and OK for me to go into the water." He looked at me strangely, apparently not understanding my joke.

When I was in the water, the guide said not to put my feet in the sand because there were stingrays hiding there that could paralyze me. He also mentioned it might be a good idea to stay away from the electric eels, since they carried 160 volts and could "light me up." He was also of the opinion the caimans would probably not be out until after nightfall. It wasn't exactly a dip in the old swimming hole. There was something about terror that added texture to the whole experience. I get a "high" whenever I recall the experience.

In May 1981, I went to China as part of a task force of 100 U.S. academic psychiatrists who were to meet with the Chinese psychiatrists.

The Chinese showed us their psychiatric hospitals, acupuncture, herbs, and other unique treatments. The wards were very well staffed with medical students, nurses, occupational therapists, and so forth. I felt they were ahead of our hospitals in giving nurture and care, but scientifically they were fifty years behind us.

We floated down the Yangtze River while our National Institutes of Mental Health psychiatrists negotiated research agreements with the Chinese psychiatrists. We climbed the Great Wall outside of Beijing, did karate *pinans* in Tian'anmen Square in Beijing, and shared a suite with the Menningers in Shanghai.

Chapter 10

I visited Arizona, and decided I wished to live in a condo in McCormick Ranch, an exclusive subdivision of the city. I got a job as a clinical director at Arizona State Hospital and a faculty appointment in the Department of Psychiatry of the University of Arizona.

At the time, leaving the children behind was not difficult for me. I felt I had a right to happiness and that I had stayed in the marriage ten years longer than I would have if it were not for them. Tiffanie, the youngest at sixteen, cried a lot when she was with me I rationalized that we would still visit each other. In retrospect, when thinking about it I cry and have the deepest regrets for going, even though I think they have all forgiven me.

I drove to Scottsdale in my 450 SL accompanied by Garrett and Tiffanie for company. I rented an apartment at the Tower at McCormick Ranch. Shortly thereafter I began my new job.

Without the superintendent's input, I was hired by the assistant director of health services, who reported to the director of health services. According to the assistant director of health services, my charge was to "shape up the bad docs."

Two of my colleagues, both émigrés from Michigan, were outstanding psychiatrists (both competent and humanistic) and I was proud to be associated with them. We felt the "Michigan connection" could improve patient care and proceeded with our plans.

Governor Babbitt was about to run for president and did not want any adverse publicity. His wish hit a serious snag when Marilyn Taylor, a reporter from the *Arizona Republic,* got herself admitted to the hospital pretending to be a patient and then wrote an exposé after she was discharged. She said that her psychiatrist was excellent but made derogatory comments about the other staff and the quality of care the patients received. Her article was on the front page of the *Republic.*

Patient advocate groups began again to clamor for change, and I had good rapport with them. I asked them to meet with me so I could hear their complaints and address them as clinical director. In this position I had completed my program initiatives and sent them to my superiors for review and approval. The patient advocates, largely parents and relatives, asked that I address them regarding my initiatives, and I agreed to do so. No one from Administration attended except a representative from the governor's office.

At the meeting the hospital chapel was packed with a loud, boisterous crowd. Unknown to me until I arrived was that TV reporters, the press, and Marilyn Taylor had all been invited. I received accolades for my initiatives, and the media carried the story.

The following is a reprint of the November 14, 1981, article from the *Arizona Republic.*

Chief Psychiatrist Proposes Reforms for State Hospital*

by Marilyn Taylor
Republic Staff

Sweeping changes, including dismantling Arizona State Hospital's violent-patient ward and reorganizing several other units, were proposed Friday by the hospital's chief psychiatrist.

Dr. Walter Turke, clinical director at the hospital, also said hospital staff should treat mental patients without seclusion and with more respect, communication and understanding.

"I believe it is malpractice to give drugs without giving love at the same time," he said.

Turke, who was hired in August, proposed the changes in a

**Arizona Republic*, November 14, 1981. Marilyn Taylor. Used with permission. Permission does not imply endorsement.

speech to a small group of mental health professionals and state officials.

He also urged a ceasefire in the "discord" between the state hospital and Maricopa County General Hospital's psychiatric staff.

"There was no grief greater than to see the amount of discord between county and state services and the disturbing myths they had about each other," Turke said.

His proposals, which, he said, county professionals helped draw up, include more cooperation between state and county systems

He also advised that private psychiatrists be permitted to practice at the State Hospital when their patients were admitted there.

Many hospital problems Turke addressed were pointed out in a series of *Arizona Republic* stories published in September. Turke and other state officials said the series helped draw attention to many problems.

Turke, who assessed the hospital for two months before drafting recommendations, said his plan has been approved by hospital administrators and will be implemented immediately.

But officials from the Arizona Department of Health Services, the agency in charge of the 344-patient hospital, have not approved the plan.

One state official said Turke's plan will not be implemented until it is reviewed by the agency.

Roberto Duran, the DHS deputy director heard Turke's plan for the first time during the speech and reacted cautiously.

Duran also said the proposals will be reviewed to determine whether the hospital has authority to implement them and whether they are in the best interests of the patients.

Turke, who gave up a private practice in Michigan to work in Arizona, said the state hospital must end its policy of "dumping" all violent patients in the "Cholla Ward."

The practice creates a "vicious cycle," he said, because violent patients are restrained and secluded, which causes them to be even more resentful and violent.

"Humane" therapy must be developed for those patients, most of whom can be moved to other wards, he said.

Only "about five or seven patients" are so dangerous that they should be separated from others, he said. Their therapy should include intensive exercise, Turke said.

The hospital should create a nursing home for its 40 elderly patients who are not mentally ill but have nowhere else to go, he said.

A greater attempt must be made to keep track of patients who leave the facility, Turke said.

"Chronic adults—psychotics—are living on the streets, living out of garbage cans," he said.

Many are former patients, he said. The hospital should keep close contact with such patients "to make sure they are adequately cared for."

Turke suggested development of "quarter houses" and halfway houses in which patients ready for release could stay until they found jobs and saved money.

He described quarter houses as places where former patients who are having financial or psychological problems could spend as many as four or five nights. Halfway houses are for patients preparing to be released.

Hospital grounds should be improved to provide patients a dignifying place to stay, Turke said.

He said he has made an arrangement with 15 Arizona State University landscape-architecture students to begin immediate improvement of hospital grounds.

"We'll have flowers and shrubs and running tracks and secluded places to meditate," Turke said.

Old, vacated hospital buildings that can be restored should be, he said, and the rest razed.

Dr. Robertson Kenner, hospital director did not attend the meeting. Turke said, however, that Kenner has approved the plan.

Turke said his proposals can be adopted without adding to the hospital's $17.1 million budget. Some proposed projects will reduce costs, he said.

The hospital's accreditation status was in jeopardy based on previous inspections. Another review team was on the way to see if the hospital had corrected the issues of concern that were brought up on the prior visit.

The program chiefs assured me that all was in order. I believed them. I had been busy with my initiatives and attempted to end the "cold war" between Maricopa County Department of Psychiatry and the state hospital, the latter being largely responsible for the problem. The former had excellent psychiatrists, including some psychoanalysts, and also had a residency training program in psychiatry.

The accrediting body again wrote up a very damaging report about the status of the hospital. The program chiefs had made virtually none of the changes they had said were done. The accrediting group gave strong support to my initiatives and told my superiors so, with great emphasis on complimenting me.

On the last day of my six-month probationary status, I was given a note by the superintendent saying I hadn't passed probation and was discharged. I contacted a prestigious law firm, and it was arranged that I would be allowed to resign rather than be fired. The patient advocates tried to reach the governor, but he would not see them. A February 26, 1982, article in the *Arizona Republic* summarized the situation:

No. 2 Official at Arizona State Hospital is Fired

A psychiatrist hired six months ago as second in command of Arizona State hospital has been fired.

Dr. Walter Turke, 51, who was employed Aug. 24 as clinical director, said Thursday he may fight the action.

Dr. Robertson Kenner, hospital superintendent, fired Turke on Wednesday.

The firing comes after Turke's attempt to make "sweeping changes" at the 300-patient institution—changes he announced in November.

Turke said he was notified of his discharge in a letter from Kenner, the superintendent.

The reason cited in the letter was his "failure to successfully complete" his six-month term as a probationary employee, Turke said.

The letter said he has no right to appeal because he was a probationary employee, he said.

"I am pursuing avenues of redress and cannot comment on them at this time," Turke said.

He also refused to discuss why he believes he was fired.

Kenner, the hospital superintendent since 1978, also refused to talk about the firing because it was a "personnel matter."

Hospital employees, however, said Turke's efforts to change

hospital procedures and patient treatment made him unpopular with staff psychiatrists and administrators.

Mike Markotic, a volunteer "patient advocate" who has an office at the hospital, said he spoke to Rep. Burton Barr, R-Phoenix, about the firing. Markotic said Barr, House majority leader, plans to investigate.

Barr was not available for comment Thursday.

"Dr. Turke is going to be missed," Markotic said. "He had the guts enough to introduce things here—some of which had been in the planning for a long time but had not been done.

"He had bright ideas and knowledge, and they [administrators and psychiatrists] felt threatened by him," Markotic said.

In November, Turke announced plans to dismantle the hospital ward for violent patients and reorganize other units.

In a public address, he also said hospital staff members should treat mental patients with fewer pills, restraints and seclusion, and more "respect, communication and understanding."

"I believe it is malpractice to give drugs without giving love at the same time," he told fellow psychiatrists and reporters.

Many of his comments moved psychiatrists to distribute a petition asking that Turke be fired.

Turke said he was told about the petition but never saw it.

He also said in November that problems at the hospital and the psychiatric unit at Maricopa County General hospital "grieved" him.

Since then, he has been credited both by county and state hospital staff members for bringing about cooperation between the two institutions.

Turke said the state hospital should keep better track of chronically mentally ill patients who are discharged.

"Chronic adults—psychotics—are living out on the streets, living out of garbage cans," Turke had said.

Some staff were enthusiastic about the suggested changes but were met with caution by officials from the state Department of Health Services.

Roberto Duran, the DHS deputy director said in November that Turke's proposal would be reviewed to determine whether the hospital had authority to implement it and whether it was in the best interest of the hospital.

Duran refused Thursday to answer questions about Turke's firing.

Turke, who was educated at the University of Iowa, also is a member of the clinical faculty at the University of Arizona.

He was paid $62,400 as clinical director for the Arizona State hospital.

I opened a part-time practice in McCormick Ranch and got privileges at Scottsdale Camelback Hospital, which also had contracts for substance abuse treatment programs for professional football players.

I was hired by Maricopa Department of Psychiatry as one of the psychotherapy supervisors for the residency training program and consulted at two satellite outpatient clinics, one in a black ghetto in South Phoenix and the other in the Hispanic ghetto in West Phoenix. Both clinics brought back memories of Fort Apache, the Bronx, but we never had any trouble. We were sure, however, to always close before dark. The patients were very grateful, and the most serious threat they posed me was offering to wash my car.

In the Hispanic satellite I worked with psychiatric nurses who were nuns. They treated the psychotic patients with holy water while I injected the haloperidol!

I also spent some time working in the Student Health Service at Arizona State University, where I was surprised at the number of coeds suffering from anorexia nervosa and bulimia.

I found it difficult to get adjusted to Arizona. I hated the incessant heat except in the winter, but the "Snowbirds" from the north came down and crowded the restaurants so it was hard to get in and driving became dangerous with many elderly drivers looking at the sights and driving so slowly.

I also detested cowboys in trucks with chewing tobacco in their blue jeans and a carbine in the back window of their pickups, constantly running red lights. I hated the seeming lack of culture and the transient nature of the people. Even the rain was a pain, always flooding when it came down too hard. I still had my roots in the Big Ten and disliked the PAC Ten. I longed for my children, the four seasons, and predictable values.

I began to go to church at the Franciscan Renewal Center on Sunday mornings and attended many of the workshops, some of which I taught. I volunteered an evening a week to see parishioners free and soon became the support person for the nuns and priests there. This was meaningful to me because they gave so much of themselves to others and I was glad to nurture them, since they had no one to share their own problems with, even though I am not Catholic.

Some weeks later I sat in the front of church at the Franciscan Renewal Center. It was extremely crowded and people were sitting in all the aisles, in front of the altar, and leaning against the walls. A former girlfriend I had been seriously dating walked in with another man. I wanted to cry, but I managed to control myself.

After the service I ran in back of the building to the garden and sat under a palm tree and sobbed so badly I couldn't drive until I calmed down more. An hour later I managed to get home to my apartment and the sobbing started again. My neighbor, a priest at the Franciscan Renewal Center, "the Casa," heard the commotion, knocked on the door wearing a San Francisco 49ers football jersey, gave me a hug, and asked me to talk about it. He listened for a long time and when I was done he gave me some very good advice, which was:

1. No alcohol—face the pain.
2. Tear up all the pictures of my ex—bury them in a hole outside the Casa prayer chapel and mark it with a rock.
3. Go to the chapel two times a day and cry there until you are bored with it.
4. Cuss her out while driving to work in your car—with the windows up!
5. Keep an anger journal—just write down angry feelings, nothing else. In about a month I would feel better.

For the next three weeks I would begin to cry in front of patients at least two times a week, but then I gradually recovered.

Some months later I began to attend a singles discussion group at the Casa being moderated by a priest. Everyone would sit on the floor, between thirty and fifty people, a topic would be decided upon, and various people would ask questions or make comments. I saw an attractive woman about sixteen to seventeen years my junior looking across the room at me, possibly attracted by my MSU sweatshirt.

We talked after the meeting, and I found out her name was Natalie. She had been divorced for a year and had a twelve-year-old son.

Natalie and I continued to go together for two years. We had common interests in sports, traveled a lot, and had a wonderful physical relationship.

On one occasion I gave a seminar out of town, about an hour-and-a-half drive out of Scottsdale. On the way back in my 450 SL she began making love to me while I was driving on the freeway with cars passing. The orgy lasted over an hour, and we ended up lost on an Indian reservation east of Scottsdale!

Natalie and I got "serious," but as we did so, her twelve-year-old son, Jason, became difficult. He demanded that Natalie stop seeing me or he would go to live with his father. Natalie felt more and more guilty and broke up with me several times but always asked me to return. I decided we would never break up permanently if I remained in Arizona. I realized if Natalie had to make a choice between me and her son it would be too difficult for her. In order to make things easier for both of us, I thought I might have to leave the state.

Before I went, though, there was a great adventure ahead of me.

Chapter 11

I had a strong need to get away and decided that I would fulfill a long-standing dream and have a South Pacific adventure. The high point of the trip was to be Papua New Guinea.

I purchased a South Pacific handbook and prepared carefully for my journey. I was immunized against polio, tetanus, typhoid, cholera, and typhus and topped it all off with three cubic centimeters of gamma globulin in my gluteus maximus just before departure. I took three types of antimalarials as Papua New Guinea had chloroquine-resistant strains of mosquitoes. I bought several pairs of rubber thongs for the mud, sturdy hiking boots, a Swiss Army knife, butane lighters to burn off the leeches, and tennis shoes for reef and river walking. I also got a snake-bite kit. Medicines included Lomotil for diarrhea, Tinaderm powder for fungal infections, calamine lotion for possible skin allergies, and Halazone tablets for water purification. I also wore a money belt.

Natalie called a few days before I left saying she loved me and did not want us to break up. The night before I left she came over and we made love most of the night. She said she'd be at the airport when I got back. My trust in her, however, did not return, and I decided to leave Scottsdale for good.

I booked a flight with Air New Zealand for late March 1984. My first stop was Tahiti and I stayed at the Beachcomber Hotel. I decided to catch *le truck,* an open rear-end conveyance popular with the natives, to Papeete for dinner.

After surveying the restaurants near the harbor, I felt it the better part of wisdom to eat at the hotel. There were a great many surly-looking people hanging around the numerous bars, looking extremely unfriendly. There was garbage lying about in most of the streets. This part of Papeete was definitely not a South Seas paradise!

Two days later I arrived at beautiful Bora Bora, staying in a thatched hut at Hotel Bora Bora. I saw spectacular vistas where many movies were shot, Marlon Brando's house (he wasn't there), and the ship from the movie *Hurricane.*

The women I saw were very beautiful. I felt uncomfortable because they talked and giggled, perhaps wondering why I was alone. The island's beauty was somewhat compromised by being infested with land crabs that would eat everything in sight—clothes, fruit, flowers, you name it. I also didn't care for the very large rats.

I then took a side trip to Mooréa, which I also enjoyed. The natives prepared a feast for me in a dirt oven and did some dances for me. The day of departure we had a violent rainstorm. I had to take a small boat, the *African Queen,* to the island where I would catch my commuter flight. The tarp covering the boat leaked, and the waves splashed inside the boat. The waters were shark-infested.

After a rather tense hour and a half, we docked. I caught my flight back to Tahiti and left for New Zealand early the following morning. After spending a day in Auckland, I left for Australia and, after twenty-four hours in the air, arrived in Sydney.

I loved beautiful and wonderful Sydney. I went to the opera house and to a tavern where they demonstrated sheep shearing, Aboriginal music, and triumphant songs about the Australians winning the America's Cup. The streets were safe, the people friendly, and the beaches beautiful. Unfortunately, Sydney is infested with red-bellied spiders, which are larger and more venomous than our black widows.

Sydney Harbor is also the spawning ground for the great white shark. My guide told me that the day before my arrival a man had been wading out to his dingy with his young son on his shoulders when a great white took the boy from his father's shoulders without harming the man.

After several days in Sydney, I took a Qantas flight to tropical Cairns, where I would get my Papua New Guinea flight in a few days. In Cairns I got to see kangaroos and koalas. My hotel was on the beach, but while I was there signs had been posted not to go in the water because of the presence of schools of venomous jellyfish. During the time I was there, there were several deaths of preadolescent children who had ignored the signs and screamed terribly as they died, unable to get free from the poisonous tentacles.

Upon my arrival at Cairns a red carpet had been rolled up to the plane. I believed I was the only American on board and, ever the optimist, jokingly wondered briefly if it was for me. Instead I found out from the stewardess that the prime minister was on board!

The highlight of my visit to Cairns was a trip in a glass-bottomed boat to the Great Barrier Reef. I also went swimming, being constantly on the lookout for reef sharks. Some of my fellow travelers laughed at me because I always wore my tennis shoes when I was in the water. I took the precaution because I was afraid to step on a stonefish with bare feet. They look like a rock, but their poison is deadly.

While I was in Cairns I reviewed the guidebooks and information that I had gathered about Papua New Guinea from the *South Pacific Handbook,* by David Stanley (Moon Publications, Chicoa, CA: 1982).

Unfortunately the Air New Guinea flight from Cairns to Port Moresby was delayed for several hours. I had cleared customs and we had to wait in a small area that was not air-conditioned. The air was humid, and there was no place to sit. The plane held about twenty passengers, most of whom were in native dress, and they were not friendly.

The flight finally arrived and we got into Port Moresby at about 10:00 P.M. I checked into the Travel Lodge in downtown Port Moresby, where I had reservations for rooms that were "posh" and comfortable. I noted the heavy security present, but I went to bed and slept well anyway.

The following morning my guide arrived and gave me a tour of the city. I noted that many of the houses had twelve-foot-high barbed-wire fences surrounding them. My guide indicated that many young men from different tribes and villages came to Port Moresby to find employment or better themselves, but their dreams usually did not come true. There was a great deal of alcohol abuse, and this led to frequent clashes of tribal warfare in Port Moresby as well as posing a threat to tourists. My guide advised me not to go out after dark because of tribal gangs.

Later that night I became bored sitting in my room and decided I would take a walk, making a circle around the hotel nor more than three city blocks away from it at any time. There was very little traffic, and the city appeared rather quiet where I was walking. I stayed in the middle of the street to avoid the numerous dark alleys. I always knew my direction to the hotel and marked each alley in my mind as best I could.

After walking for about twenty minutes, I noted a group of nationals ahead of me, about four or five men, and they appeared to be carrying machetes and axes. I turned around and saw a similar group in back of me. I walked slowly toward the group in back of me since they were farther away. Suddenly I dashed at top speed down an alley I had remembered that would take me back to the lodge. I arrived safely and that was the last night I went out at Port Moresby!

I asked my guide to take me to a secluded beach where I could enjoy a day of rest before pushing on to more arduous adventures inland. We drove along a highway that faced the Coral Sea and went toward the Gulf of Papua. We found an ideal spot, and my guide indicated he had some business to take care of and would return in the late afternoon. He advised me that the Coral Sea was shark-infested because, following the battle of the Coral Sea, they had feasted so well on the sailors and airmen who had drowned that the species had thrived. He also warned me about sea snakes, which were aggressive and poisonous.

I had a most pleasant day and was completely relaxed. Suddenly I noticed a long, dark shape coming toward me about a city block away. I decided to begin walking toward the highway some distance through the beach grass. To my horror, the shape kept getting closer and soon began to look like a crocodile. As I began to run I discovered the damn thing was chasing me!

When I got to the road, a government vehicle approached and I jumped in front of it, waving my arms for them to stop. I got a ride back to Port Moresby, and when I was finally in my hotel room I dug out my South Papua guidebook. I found out that saltwater crocodiles grow up to thirty feet in length and can move up to forty miles per hour! Later on a Qantas flight to Fiji I read an article in their flight magazine about saltwater crocodiles. They are highly territorial and not infrequently attack small boats that they may see as rivals . . . and people on the beach.

The following day I arranged a trip to the Sepik River, where, with a new guide and from a dugout canoe, we shined the light of a lantern into the eyes of crocodiles to see the yellow-orange color. Very exciting, even though they appeared nonaggressive toward us and were probably not the saltwater version!

The next stop on the journey was to a frontier town called Mount Hagan, which at the time had been in existence only about fifteen years. My guide told me there had been six deaths in the town from tribal warfare the week before. Somehow I still felt safe in Mount Hagan, where I feasted on taro root, taro leaf spinach, baked yams, sweet potatoes, tapioca root, baked breadfruit, wild pumpkin with coconut, roast pork, tropical fruits, sweet corn, cucumbers, sago, tomatoes, tall grass ("pit pit"), and raw peanuts. I had previously eaten crocodile meat barbecued with sauce. The taste was somewhat like chicken.

My guide took me hiking into the bush outside Mount Hagen. He was small of stature but very strong. He wore what resembled Marine Corps fatigues and boots. He told me his father had been killed in a tribal war and, according to custom, he had killed a member of that tribe as "payback." He realized that members of that tribe were now looking for him and he surmised he would probably not live very long.

After a day in the bush, we returned very tired to the Highlander Lodge. To my surprise, there was a TV in the bar where a group of Australian anthropologists were watching the final minutes of the NIT basketball championship via satellite. Michigan was in the process of beating Notre Dame. I sang a chorus of "Hail to the Victors" and taught them to sing it as well. They bought me a couple of drinks, and we had a most enjoyable evening.

My guide had a four-wheel-drive vehicle that was able to traverse some of the formidable roads in the Highlands. On one occasion as we traveled, the road was blocked with nationals carrying axes, clubs, and knives. There were about seven men, who looked menacing. I decided not to make eye contact. My guide talked to them in "pidgin" for about fifteen minutes, which felt like an eternity, and then they let us pass. My guide pretended not to hear my questions and didn't answer them. I was pleased to be safe and let the matter drop.

My guide showed me a village that had been burned to the ground and was now desolate. All the people had been murdered as part of a "payback". Later a missionary told me that a group of Japanese tourists had been stopped in a similar fashion as we just had and robbed. However, to the nationals' surprise, the Japanese used karate on the natives when they let their guard down! The missionary noted that the witch doctors were quite hostile toward the missionaries' activities and they were sometimes threatened and stoned.

I asked my guide about cemeteries, of which I had seen none. He stated that if his ten-year-old daughter died, she would not be buried. "William" (loose translation) indicated he would instead invite the entire family, cut the girl up in little pieces, and eat her, saving one hand (at the wrist) for a necklace. I almost lost my lunch! They believed that dead people are in the "spirit world" and therefore not completely gone.

On the way to Kundiawa we stopped in the village of Chief Peni and I took Polaroid pictures of him and his family. He asked me to stay with him for a visit after I gave him the pictures. The renowned Asaro mudmen with their fearsome masks lived in this area. They did a ghostlike dance that had originated when the people were driven into the river during a battle. When they emerged, covered with clay, their enemies thought they were evil spirits and fled.

They demonstrated their prowess with bow and arrow by shooting at a wooden post. One arrow missed the post and went into a grass hut, killing a dog inside. The chief fed me roasted bat. Apparently, when the bats were away feeding, the trunk of the tree where they lived was cut almost entirely through. Later while the bats slept, the tree was felled and the bats were then clubbed to death and roasted.

After the mudmen had finished their slow, ghostlike dances, I did a shotokan karate *pinan* for them, a dance utilizing ritualized movements that were lethal, symbolically dealing with a large number of attacking enemies.

We then went on to Kundiawa, a town of somewhat over four thousand inhabitants located in the center of Chimbu Province, created out of the Eastern Highlands in 1966. The *South Pacific Handbook* states: "Be careful, the place is rowdy and tough. If you want to experience this side of Papua New Guinea, try hanging around the hotel on Friday night, but make out your will first. Unless you know somebody, it's better to move on before nightfall."

I was booked into the Chimbu Lodge, but my guide could not stay there. I noted the twelve-foot-high barbed-wire fence that surrounded the place.

There had been a great commotion when the guide and I first entered town. The police cars were just leaving, and my guide surmised that there was a tribal war taking place outside town.

We stopped briefly in town to buy some pop, but everyone stared at us and appeared to be not only unfriendly, but angry. The guide talked to the shop owner and found out that four Australians had been in town and the two women in the group had worn short shorts. The natives felt they were taunting them and began to stone the people. The Australians had apparently left town in a hurry.

At dusk, wearing masks and knives and chanting, a dozen men marched on the fence surrounding our hotel. Hotel security had long bamboo poles they intended to use to prevent the nationals from climbing the high barbed-wire fence. I was told to lock myself in my room, but I was sufficiently frightened that I put my valuables in a plastic bag, took a bamboo rod to use as an airway, and jumped into the outdoor pool covered by a green slime. When I felt it was safe, I returned to my room. I was delighted to see my guide the next day and learned that the barbed-wire fence had not been bridged during the night. We began driving on the road to Goroka.

My guide told me that wealth was based upon the number of wives and pigs that one had. Cooking was done inside the grass hut, while lovemaking took place in the bush. Women did all the work. Men guarded them, loafed, and drank.

As we drove on, the guide stopped the Jeep and we had a

tough climb up a mountain. Before the climb, in the valley, I was bitten by several mosquitoes the size of flies. Near the top of the mountain was an opening about two and one-half feet square. My guide said bodies from tribal wars were thrown in there. The pit was about twenty feet by twenty feet and said to be about a hundred feet deep. The skeletons were covered with blankets to keep "the living spirits warm."

We then went on to Goroka, where I learned there were twelve cases of kiru, a viral disease of the brain contracted by cannibalism. My guide told me what had happened to the young Rockefeller; he knew the tribe that ate him!

It became time to leave, and I bade my guide, William, a fond farewell and tipped him generously. My Air Niugini flight was uneventful, except I had to search for over an hour for my suitcase in the Port Moresby airport. I caught a Qantas flight in Cairns and started on the way home via Fiji, a friendly and safe island. On my arrival in Fiji I was transported to the elegant and comfortable Regent of Fiji, just outside Nandi Town. All the employees greeted you with a smile and, "Bula," i.e., "Have a nice day." The Regent had a bar in the middle of the swimming pool!

I was surprised to see a Hindu temple near Nandi Town until I saw that East Indians owned most of the tourist shops there. I visited the Fiji historical museum and purchased a facsimile of an authentic cannibal fork used for eating liver, pancreas, and kidneys. Later when visiting the outer islands, I purchased a Fiji warrior club, which is used in striking an enemy to the ground and then choking the person with the notch to fit the throat.

The people were very friendly and there were many Methodists among them. While I was there, I swam in the Blue Lagoon, where the movie starring Jean Simmons was shot. We swam into a large limestone cavern and then had to swim underwater to get into the second inner cave. I still wore my tennis shoes to avoid stepping on any poisonous stonefish.

I entered into frequent conversations with one of the hotel employees and gave him an MSU sweatshirt on departure. He invited me to his home to have ceremonial kava with his family and friends Upon my arrival I learned that I was the guest of honor!

Kava comes from the green root of the pepper plant. The ritual is performed with all due seriousness seated on floor mats. The root is chewed until it is the right consistency and then mixed with water in the *tanoa*. The pulp is shaped into a ball, then kneaded and strained through hibiscus fibers to squeeze the juices into the *tanoa*. When the drink was of the right consistency it was drunk out of a half coconut shell dipped into the bowl. The drinker claps once when offered the bowl and three times after drinking.

The ceremony began at 6:00 P.M., and my Air New Zealand flight was to depart at 9:00, with boarding at about 8:00 P.M. Word was received that my flight was delayed by bad weather for another two hours, so the party continued till nine. I was then returned to await transport to my flight. I had to check out of my room, so I sat on a couch outside the dining room, which had an adjacent bar with music. Unfortunately, this area was open to the outside and the mosquitoes loved psychiatrists' blood.

My Air New Zealand flight didn't take off until 4:45 because of severe weather, so when we got into LA I found my connecting flight to Phoenix had already left. I was put up in a hotel for departure the next day home.

Natalie could not be reached, so I called her after I got back home. We had a wonderful reunion, but Jason was still threatening Natalie with living with his father and I knew it was time to leave. I interviewed with the Universities of Georgia, Alabama, South Carolina and South Dakota, finally accepting a position with the latter. I left Phoenix in June of 1985 at four in the morning.

It appears that I took significant risks during this adventure, but I was, however, streetwise in taking care of myself, having been raised in Brooklyn. If you can survive the streets of New York, crocodiles and cannibals are not as intimidating. With my karate training I may have carried myself differently than those who become victims. The trip raised me self-esteem and still gives me "highs" when I recapture it with memories and my photo album.

Chapter 12

Things weren't over with Natalie though, I discovered. She called to tell me she had seriously thought of giving custody of Jason to her husband and also might be willing to leave Arizona to be with me in Sioux Falls, where I was to be assistant professor in the Department of Psychiatry, School of Medicine, at the University of South Dakota. I was also to be director of the Inpatient Teaching Unit for the University of South Dakota medical students.

Somewhere along the way, though, Natalie had a change of heart and told me she couldn't leave her son after all. Tired of the emotional trauma she was causing me, I got an unlisted phone number so that I wouldn't have to talk to her again. She found out where I worked from the American Medical Association, and then my secretary started getting "emergency" phone calls from Natalie begging me to come back to Arizona. These calls gradually became less frequent over the next year.

During this time I continued to see patients in addition to my teaching duties. As always, there were many interesting moments.

While I was making inpatient rounds for the Department of Psychiatry at McKennan Hospital, a newly admitted manic patient approached me at the nursing station. He was a patient of another faculty member.

"I'm being persecuted by the devil!" the patient shouted at me. "And he's butt fucking me too!"

The nurses, some of them nuns, began to pay attention.

"Is the feeling in your rectum cold?" I asked him.

"No. Why?" he said.

"It can't be the devil invading your backside," I reassured him. "I heard that he is supposed to have a cold penis."

I told the patient that we would protect him and at the same time regulated his lithium. He was discharged a week later by his faculty psychiatrist.

Approximately two months after that I was again making weekend rounds when I looked up from my charts at the nurses' station and spotted the man, recently readmitted. I casually approached him.

"Still having trouble with the devil?" I said.

"He's not messing with me anymore, but you'd better be careful," he warned me.

"Why?" I said.

"Because the devil told me he was coming after you now."

I shrugged and said, "Any time I feel something cold in my rectum, I really get angry!"

"Why?" he said.

"Insufficient foreplay," I said with a straight face.

The patient laughed and the nurses turned bright red. They later reported the incident to the board of trustees. Personally, I was proud of a great therapeutic comment.

I was asked to be the director of the new residency training program in psychiatry, in addition to my previously mentioned duties. I asked to be promoted to associate professor, and the Department of Psychiatry agreed, as did the Medical School and the dean. The president of the University rejected the promotion on the basis of lack of research and publications. The president "accepted" my resignation and bid me farewell.

South Dakota was not exactly a high point in my social life. I had only one date, and that was a blind one. One of the faculty psychologists at the university told me he knew of a very attractive single woman who was well educated and would be just right for me. I agreed to go out with her, and the woman called me to set up a time to get together. We met for a drink at a local restaurant on Halloween Eve. She was very attractive, charming, and intelligent. After the second drink, however, she told me of several hospitalizations for bipolar disorder, manic type. I noticed my hand start to tremble. She said she was going to a costume party later. "I'm going with orange hair as a garbage bag. Should I wear my combat boots?" I looked at my watch, said I had an urgent engagement, and left there in great haste!

Leaving Sioux Falls, I interviewed at MSU and got a full-time faculty appointment. I had three other offers, two with community mental health centers and one with Bay Medical Center. I was appointed associate clinical professor and became the coordinator of the clerkships in psychiatry on the MSU Saginaw campus. As a result I brought the medical students to Bay Medical Center's Psychiatric Unit, where i was medical director and Associate Clinical Professor in the Department of Psychiatry at MSU.

An interesting thing about my position at Bay Medical Center was that I was the medical director of the Psychiatric Unit and the clinical director of Bay-Arenac Community Mental health, which occupied the second floor of the N.H. Annex. A conflict was created for me in my dual role, since the community mental health philosophy centers around keeping patients out of the hospital as much as possible while the psych unit needed to keep its beds full. I did my job, perhaps too well, in keeping patients out, which caused resentment from the BMC administration.

To complicate matters more, an R.N., who was working on her master's degree, was administratively in charge of the unit and all the nurses, psychologists, OTs, social workers, etc., reported directly to her. She was a behaviorist and somewhat uncomfortable with my psychodynamic orientation. The nurses, who had formerly done considerable therapy, were now preempted to a degree by the medical students, which led to further conflict. The charge nurse was very close to the director of nursing, as well as the BMC CEO. I was closer in philosophy with the executive director of the community mental health center.

Several months later I received a letter from the CEO stating that my position was being phased out due to a "reorganization." I was greatly relieved but also depressed and angry. In retrospect, it seems that it was the best thing that ever happened to me, because it brought me to Saginaw Cooperative Hospitals (the Saginaw campus of MSU), the best place I have ever worked, with the nicest people.

Chapter 13

There has been only one "significant other" since returning to Michigan but that did not work out after a year, and so, generally speaking, I have become content with my bachelorhood. My days have taken on a pleasant, predictable rhythm, which I find comforting although lacking in any serious passion. I live in a beautiful semi-rural area north of Saginaw. There are several lakes and a river encompassing the area where fish and other wildlife abound.

My neighborhood is inhabited by somewhat older people, half of whom are comfortably retired and whose children return occasionally with grandchildren in tow. There is virtually no traffic disturbing the area. The neighborhood organization is strong. During football season, college flags fly from various residences. There is a private security patrol that is very active, while the neighborhood watch is formidable due to the many retired people living there.

My residence has twenty-three hundred square feet, which accommodates two guest bedrooms, a guest bathroom, a large living room that extends into a dining room, an adequate kitchen, a two-car garage, and a solarium that houses sago palms, rubber trees, and hibiscus plants. The lengthy hallway leading from the front door has family and children's photos, along with those of old girlfriends and letters and certificates of commendation (navy, academic, karate, etc.). There are four University of Iowa lamps illuminating the pictures of Hayden Fry, the head football coach, Kinnick Stadium, football calendars, and Iowa floor mats. The Iowa flag flies on the pole just outside the front door.

Erikson has written that the task of life at my age is a struggle between integrity and despair. Integrity means you are satisfied with the way you have lived your life, achieved your goals, and done all the things you wanted to do. Therefore, dying is not scary. Despair reflects an unfulfilled life with missed opportunities. Depression and fear of death then prevail.

My home reflects me, my travels, achievements, and treasured memories that make me happy when I reminisce. Hundreds of videos and CDs are displayed in six storage towers in the living room. Many of the videos are emotionally meaningful films I grew up with, along with films I use to teach psychodynamics to MSU students who come to my home four evenings during each eight-week clerkship for Psychiatry Club, with Pepsi and pizza.

I frequently spend in excess of fifty hours a week at the office seeing patients. Medical students are with me who do the clinical work in my presence. The vast majority of patients don't object. I enjoy my work immensely, but when I leave the office I don't have much energy left or interest in talking with others. I believe this may have caused at least one relationship to end. Thursdays are twelve-hour days at the office, and my ex-girlfriend often wanted to go out on the town on Friday nights while I was still recovering from the previous night. Also, I have an "addiction" to Big Ten and Detroit Lions football. Finding a girlfriend who has the same interests is a formidable task.

My life has taken on a comfortable routine that I enjoy. The workdays have a rhythm to them that works well for me. I get up at 5:45 A.M., drink a cup of instant coffee, and do fifteen to twenty minutes of transcendental meditation. I then shave, shower, dress, feed my green iguana, Thor, who lives in a huge custom-made terrarium, then eat some cereal and head for the office in Saginaw. I'm usually there by 7:00 to 7:15 A.M. so I can get the charts ready to see the day's patients beginning at 8:00.

From 8:00 to 5:00 I see patients, teach students, and go to administrative and academic meetings, taking time out at lunchtime for a cup of instant soup in the office and twenty minutes of meditation. I also walk the basement halls for aerobic exercise during the cold weather.

I'm usually home by 5:30 except for nights when I have group meetings or MSU committee meetings in East Lansing, about ninety miles away. I take out my contacts, put on my glasses, check out the mail, say hi to Thor, get into my Iowa or MSU sweatshirt and jeans, and have dinner in front of the TV. I catch the 6:00 local news, the 6:30 NBC national news with Tom Brokaw (because he's also a University of Iowa grad), then take my pick of the evening's offerings on my fifty-channel TV. I prefer HBO, Showtime, the Movie Channel, Cinemax, Encore, and sports.

At 11:30 I turn in after catching the local news and weather report.

Weekends are naturally different but just as enjoyable for me. I'm usually up by 7:00 A.M. and off to the store for the week's groceries and supplies. I feed Thor, water the plants, clean up the condo, write checks, and answer correspondence. After an hour's walk through some of the nature trails around the condo, I watch two Big Ten football games while grabbing a sandwich.

In the evening I'll fix something small to eat and watch TV or videos. I'm uncomfortable going out to movies, bars, or dinner alone. I see enough of the external world at the frequent academic meetings out of town and the extensive vacations I plan each year.

I stay in close contact with my children, spending holidays with them, seeing them once a month, and talking to them every Sunday morning. My son, son-in-law, and I watch all the Bowl games together and bet to see who makes the best choices in order to win the battered "Spartan Cup" for the coming year—a wonderful prize indeed!

On Sundays I may go to church or for a drive, making sure I'm home in time for any games during pro-football season.

I get a great deal of satisfaction from my teaching responsibilities with the MSU students. My basic philosophy is to be a good role model for them. I do the same things I want them to do and then explain why I did them. I challenge them to ask questions, and then I focus on the more meaningful ones. I try to demonstrate good psychiatric skills effectively and then get the students actively involved with the patients. I allow them to work up new patients and follow their progress in treatment. Students help run the Psychopharmacology Clinic and participate in two ongoing therapy groups. We discuss each patient before he/she arrives, thinking about what difficulties we might encounter, what drugs are involved and how they work, along with pre- and postgroup discussions of the therapy sessions they were involved in.

I tell the students what to look for, then get them to commit the analytical steps to memory. I'll watch the students interact with the patient and prompt them if they miss asking important questions or don't know how to proceed.

Chapter 14

I find it interesting that in writing my memoirs I did not mention the deaths of my parents and sister, an omission I need to correct.

In 1966 at age 55 I received a call from my father informing me that my mother had died of a massive cerebral hemorrhage during a prayer meeting. The hemorrhage was undoubtedly caused by her hypertension. I called a psychiatrist friend, Herb Gross, and asked him if he would cover my practice while I flew East. I cried for my mother for the first time that I could recall. I cried again while making my airline reservations.

My sister, Frieda, was there in New York, and while we were never very close, we became more so during this time of mourning. My father told me it was not necessary to mourn, as Mother was "already in paradise." My father stood next to the coffin at the burial site, and when the minister completed his message Father began to deliver an emotional fire-and-brimstone sermon, which continued at least twenty minutes. My sister and I were embarrassed and angry at the inappropriateness of his behavior and it brought Frieda and me closer. It was difficult to grieve for my mother. I had so many mixed feelings. I don't think I did a good job of it.

I was in therapy with a patient in my Traverse city office when my father called a second time. He was crying and simply said, "We lost Frieda." I excused my patient and Father went on to tell me that my sister had crossed the road, turned over in a ditch, and hit a tree on a sunny day with no traffic around. There were no skid marks on the road. My father had refused an autopsy, which made me unhappy. In addition, I was unable to get a flight East from Traverse City and missed the funeral. My sister and her husband had four daughters, and there were rumors of marital discord and conflicts about how to raise the children. I considered the possibility of suicide but felt a ruptured aneurysm in the brain was more likely, as my sister had labile hypertension.

I visited her grave a month later and grieved that we had never been closer.

I was lecturing to a group of Michigan State medical students when I was asked to take an emergency phone call in '88. My niece was on the phone saying that my father had just had a massive heart attack and had been pronounced dead. I dismissed my class and told the assistant dean that I was going to take a week off. I spent the day ruminating as to whether I could go to the funeral. My father had moved to Chapel Hill, North Carolina, to live with my niece and her husband. I was informed that a church service had been set and that a large number of Father's friends and admirers would be there. I decided I could not handle this and so informed my niece. I sent a money order to pay all expenses but informed my niece that I planned to grieve alone after I had finished what I knew I had to do.

I spent a week at home doing nothing but writing a forty-five-page letter to my father. No tears were shed until I received a hand-written note and card from Norb Enzer, the chairperson of the MSU Department of Psychiatry. I began to sob and continued off and on for several days. Some of my tears were for Father, but most were for me. Norb, whom I have known for nearly a quarter of a century, had demonstrated a sensitivity and caring for me that I had never experienced with my father.

I instructed that Father's ashes be sent to me and buried them under my favorite crimson maple tree. I read my letter to my father there, and for the first time I was able to cry for him, recognizing that he had parents, too. I also realized that he had loved me in the only way in which he was able.

Chapter 15

I have been fortunate to go through life with good health. However, in August of 1994 I developed palpitations and an irregular heartbeat, primarily during sleep, which made me feel as though I were dying. I consulted my personal physician and was put on a monitor and a diagnosis of paroxysmal tachycardia was made. My health habits were good, and the only emotional stressor that I was aware of was that the Promotions and Tenure Committee of the Department of Psychiatry was reviewing my request for promotion to clinical professor. The chairperson of this committee had a tragedy in his family that took him away from campus. I also grieved over this loss.

I consulted an eminent cardiologist whom I knew as a real "mensch" and had a complete cardiac workup. The same diagnosis was made and my arrhythmia was "essentially benign." I was placed on Tanbocor, 100 milligrams twice a day, which terminated the arrhythmia.

During this time I had also applied for an American Medical Association insurance policy of $100,000, which would pay off my condominium mortgage in the event of my death. An R.N. came to my office to conduct an examination. Several weeks went by and then I received a letter of rejection! There was a large red circle around PSA (prostate specific antigen). I had been feeling absolute wonderful after seeing Dr. Kahn and now I became frightened. Prostate cancer at age sixty-four!

I had no symptoms of any kind, but I made an appointment with a prominent urologist, Joseph Aquilina, M.D., since there is a great deal of difference between a prostate exam from a family practitioner and from a urologist. This knowledge did nothing to minimize the pain from Dr. Aquilina's expert probings.

Dr. Aquilina confirmed that I did have prostate cancer and that radical surgery would be the best treatment at my age. I was scheduled for a repeat PSA, as well as an ultrasound and a prostate biopsy. I also had the medical library do a literature search for me about prostate cancer so that I could be clinically informed. I had decided that the quality of life was more important than the length and that I would choose a conservative therapy that would allow me to continue teaching without dribbling urine all the way to East Lansing. From the literature search I did discover that the survival rate for five to ten years is 93 percent with surgery, 83 percent with radiation therapy, and 89 percent by doing nothing!

I had been instructed by my urologist to take a Fleet's enema an hour before the ultrasound, so I went to St. Luke's Hospital's apothecary shop to buy it. Unfortunately, there were a lot of people there at the time and when I whispered to the pharmacist, "Can I give this to myself?" everyone started laughing. It may be a question only a psychiatrist could ask. After taking the enema home with me, I decided I could not give the enema correctly, so I had a physician's assistant student help me.

I checked in at St. Mary's Hospital as an outpatient for the ultrasound. I was greeted by a Hispanic-American technician who relaxed me with casual conversation and then explained how she would do the examination and how the probe would be placed in my rectum. Some of my anxiety disappeared because I realized I was in the hands of a very competent person. I even experienced a feeling of mild pleasure during the rectal probing.

She said that everything looked good, but the films would have to be read by a radiologist and by my urologist. Dr. Aquilina's son came to do my biopsy. We chatted pleasantly as he told me he would be taking three pieces from each lobe of my prostate. The needle taking the specimens sounded like a staple gun and felt something like someone was pinching me on the butt. The younger Aquilina answered my questions about conservative therapies, and I felt more relieved.

I had come to the hospital in my Michigan State Medicine sweatshirt and my University of Iowa Hawkeye walking shoes, so I knew I was well protected by my personal talismans. Superstition and psychiatry are not necessarily mutually exclusive.

I asked myself how I felt about the possibility of dying at the age of sixty-four. I decided that I had accomplished most of my goals in life, traveled all over the world, had great adventures, had been loved by several women, and was proud of my children and grandchildren. I thought dying could be done without regrets. It seems that dying must indeed be terrifying for those poor souls who have never lived, yet go through life without daring to live the great adventures and take risks in loving, caring, and being brave.

Someone asked if I feared death. I replied, "If I get my promotion to professor, the rest will be gravy."

It was interesting to note that on the morning I was having my outpatient tests, my four-foot-long male iguana, Thor, found himself without food because I had left his romaine lettuce, carrots, parsley, and banana slices on the kitchen counter. When I came home I saw that the eight-foot-by-six-foot terrarium where he hangs out was empty. Nothing appeared to be amiss, which seemed strange, since I thought the house would likely be trashed. I closed the doors to each room and started in the back of each one, searching with a flashlight. No iguana to be seen! On my way back to the terrarium I noticed Thor perched on the top branch of my artificial palm tree. He allowed me to pick him up, but as we got closer to the terrarium he suddenly tried to bite me and dig his claws into me while snapping his tail. I dropped him in and closed the screen, and he went berserk, hitting his tail angrily against the glass for something like five minutes. He avoided me for twenty-four hours but then allowed me, gradually, to pet him again.

I consulted Joseph C. Cerny, M.D., clinical professor of urology at the University of Michigan and chairman of the urology department at Henry Ford Hospital in Detroit. Dr. Cerny and I had instant rapport, and a mutual trust and respect developed. After several outpatient visits, I underwent laparoscopic pelvic node sampling and interstial I-125 placement on February 1. The procedures went extremely well. The lymph nodes were negative. Dr. Khil, the radiation oncologist (who was also wonderful), placed a total of sixty-eight seeds in the prostate, going through the scrotum, with a CT computer simulation modeling technique. A total of thirty-four millicuries were delivered. The following morning I was feeling quite well and walked about in my room, as I was very radioactive. I ate and slept well, and my Foley catheter was removed on February 4 and I was discharged from Henry Ford Hospital. I returned to my regular duties on February 9 with my only symptom being urinary frequency and some blood in my urine.

My pubic hair had been shaved, and my scrotum was an exquisite purple. I had a fleeting fantasy that I could be the centerfold in *Playgirl.* I am sure this would have been exotic and/or erotic. However, this fantasy was worth a few laughs. At the present time I am feeling well and have no symptoms, and Joe feels my life expectancy is the same as his: eighty-one. I am working out with my shotokan karate again, doing *wazas* and *pinions,* which involve offensive and defensive strikes. I also have a *makiwara* (punching board) in my garage.

I continue to serve on the following committees:

1. Medical Student Education Committee, East Lansing.
2. Pre-Matriculation Subsidiary Committee (East Lansing), which consists of the ABLE Committee, recruiting people of color into medical school and providing them with nurturing and ongoing support so that they will graduate and, we hope, return to their communities to practice medicine. The second component of this committee is the Medical Scholar Program, which recruits people with very high IQs and gives them unique opportunities in growth while in premed and in medical school. We are making every effort to attract people of color. Women are equally represented in medical school with men.
3. Program Director's Meeting, Saginaw campus, weekly.
4. Academic Affairs Committee, Saginaw campus, monthly.
5. Continuing Education Committee, Saginaw campus.
6. Saginaw County Medical Society Ethics Committee, meeting as needed.
7. Ethics Committee, Saginaw campus; and arrange for four presentations a year for CME credit.
8. Spirituality and Human Values in Medicine Committee,

Saginaw campus—there are also four presentations a year with the general public invited.

I continue my memberships in the American Medical Association, Michigan Psychiatric Society, American Psychiatric Association, Directors of Medical Student Education in Psychiatry, Association for Academic Psychiatry, Michigan State Medical Society, and Saginaw County Medical Society.

In January of this year my promotion to clinical professor was reified. I plan on teaching another five years, as I enjoy being a clinical professor!

Commencement for the Class of 1995 of the College of Human Medicine, Michigan State University took place at the Wharton Center for Performing Arts on May 13th. The night before at the university club there was an awards banquet hosted by the Minority Medical Student Association, Graduating Class of '95. My daughter, son, and their spouses attended with my grandchildren, Lindsey and Shani. I received an award for "Outstanding and Dedicated Service" to minority medical students. Lindsey and Shani, both six years old, accompanied me to the podium to receive the award. The following day at commencement I received the "Excellence in Teaching Award" from the graduating class. Mark Greenwell, a graduating senior going into psychiatry, reviewed highlights of my life and handed me the award with a hug.

I stated: "I am especially pleased to be here this morning to honor the best class I have ever taught in thirty-eight years of being a psychiatrist and role model for medical students.

"As I walk down memory lande some years from now, I will think of each of you—shed a tear—and then smile as I remember that great senior class of '95 . . . "

Four months after prostate treatment at Henry Ford Hospital in Detroit, my P.S.A. went from 10.6 before treatment to 1.4, which is in the normal range; in the four months thereafter the P.S.A. dropped to 0.5. It appears I shall survive!

Post Script I

After the proofs of my book were received, I realized that I had left out something important, i.e., group therapy. I felt it was important for my readers to become familiar with this therapeutic modality. The patients in the dialogue are composites of real patients. The place is Los Angeles and the time is the 60's.

Over the years I have found a great deal of success treating patients in group settings. I often incorporate the teaching process along with the patient care. During each academic year, I have medical students evaluate new patients; at which time we identify those people who might be likely candidates for group therapy. I always include the students in group therapy, which lasts an hour and a half, and sessions are weekly.

The group process works in the following manner:

1. Each patient is required to share with the fellow group members:
   a. The reasons for coming to the group.
   b. What they hope to achieve.
   c. Significant life stressors and conflicts.
2. Each person shares ongoing events in their life and their feelings.
3. Feedback comes from the members as to their:
   a. Judgment in resolving specific programs.
   b. Intensity of feelings or lack thereof in relationship to significant others.
   c. Capacity for emotional intimacy with others.
   d. Progress toward emotional growth and well-being.
4. Some of the subjects we discuss are: loneliness, intimacy, hostility, love, communication, respect, trust, and gender issues.

Each member is required to sign a contract that contains the Group Rules:

I agree to abide by the following rules:

1. I will respect and keep confidential what my fellow group members share with me.

2. I will honestly express my feelings to the best of my ability as they arise, including feelings about the doctor.

3. I will express my feelings in words rather than in actions.

4. I agree that I will not engage in outside relationships with any of the group members.

5. I agree to be punctual and regular in attendance for my own benefit and the other members of the group. I will not bring food or beverages to therapy.

6. I will share with the group, in advance, at the beginning of the session, any unavoidable absences in the near future and the reason for such absence. In the event that an emergency occurs, I will leave a brief message with the secretary or on the answering machine, giving the reason for the absence. If the doctor is free, I will talk with him directly.

7. I agree to pay the full fee for any session missed if a majority of the group members, including the doctor, feel that the absence occurred because I wished to avoid a painful emotional issue or the reason for the absence was not as important as group attendance. I understand that missed sessions will not be billed to the insurance company.

8. I understand that violation of the group rules may be grounds for immediate dismissal from the group.

The following scenario is fairly representative of many of the groups I have worked with over the years. Patients' lives encompass a broad spectrum of socio-economic backgrounds. Their common denominator is their inability to express their emotions and to reach contentment with who and what they are. They come to us seeking a solution when the solution is frequently within themselves.

The group:

Lance–a primary care physician
Mary–executive secretary for a casting studio
Bill–Methodist minister
Melissa–an actress on a soap opera
Rich–a movie executive
Jody–a registered nurse
Maury–Ph.D. psychologist
Rob–university assistant professor
Mitch–telecommunications

Group Therapy Dialogue

Lance: I need to talk. I'm very depressed, all burned out! I can't take it anymore. I need to do something else with my life but I don't know what. My patients are so demanding—it's like they are eating me up!

Mary: Why do you push yourself so hard?

Lance: It's hard to say no to people—I try to be perfect.

Bill: Is it true that you're not married?

Lance: I'm gay. I keep dreaming about being a male model in New York. I could make big bucks and run with the rich and famous. I still have my figure and looks. I could live with a lot of rich guys, but not just for the money, expensive clothes, care and presents. I really would have to like them. I'm really a great lover. I think I could be innovative and exciting. I could really turn them on.

Rich (interrupting): Damn it. Lance, I've heard this story of yours at least a half dozen times since I've been with you in the group and quite frankly I'm bored with it. I think you bring up this depression stuff now so that you can get center stage. You're wasting the group's time!

Bill: I know that you're gay, Lance, and I really am uncomfortable around you. I preach sermons against homosexuality. The whole subject makes me a little sick . . .

Melissa: You're such a pious bastard, Bill, and I really don't especially like you. You've got that holier-than-thou attitude. I can't stand it when you sound like you're giving a sermon in here.

Bill: I felt you didn't like me from the start but I didn't know why. I thought you just didn't like men . . . I want to share with the group that I'm disenchanted with the church. People are always making demands on me, too. There's no time for my family. Church politics bother me and I always have to please the people who tithe. My marriage isn't so great and my wife hates the hours I am away from home. Damn it! (He begins to cry.)

Melissa: I think I like you a lot better right now, Bill. I guess you are human.

Bill: Thanks, Melissa. (Wipes away tears.)

John—medical student: Lance looks very depressed. I'd like us to get back to him. Have you thought about killing yourself, Lance?

Lance: I think about it a lot but I've never tried it or made a plan. That fucking Rich used to be my friend but now he makes snide comments about me. He should talk. God damn alcoholic who can't handle retiring from MGM where he was a big shot. He got depressed when his wife divorced him and took half his money and he can't cope with it.

Melissa: I need some time. I'm again seeing the guy that stood me up at the altar. He's so handsome that I can't resist him. I think he's a loser—he's still seeing his ex-wife.

Jody: That really sounds so self-destructive, Melissa. I remember that you were so suicidal when he left you at the altar, that you were in the hospital for a week until you could deal with your hate for him. And now you're seeing him again?

Melissa: I know it sounds stupid, Jody. Thanks for reminding me! I'd like to change the subject, if you don't mind. You know how I have a crush on Rob over there. I really like him a lot. I know we can't see each other since we're both in the group. But, I must tell you that I've lost all my respect for you, Rob. I saw you in the Whiskey a Go-Go last Friday but you didn't see me. You were pie-eyed and scanning all the women in the bar. You looked like a jerk, all dressed up and on the prowl. I can't respect you anymore.

Rob (embarrassed): I wasn't pie-eyed. I just wanted to see where the action was and have a few drinks. I've got about eight to ten women who want to go out with me; who come up to me and the Whiskey and give me their phone number and sometimes a condom!

Maury: Rob, didn't you tell us you've been seeing a wonderful woman in LaJolla for two years now? The one with three kids? Does she know about this other side of you?

Rob: No she doesn't. I haven't followed through with any of these offers, yet. The thought of making love to all these other women is too exciting to resist.

Jean—medical student: Now I can understand why you have panic attacks, Rob. (Group members laugh.) Also, you know that you agreed that you would abstain from alcohol in accordance with the group rules!

Rob (embarrassed again—nods affirmatively): I've been under a lot of pressure at work. My research project that I've been working on for five years is being soundly criticized. My students—some of them—criticize my teaching—I may not get promoted to associate professor! (tearing up.)

Maury: Thanks for sharing that, Rob. I really respect you for trusting us with your tears.

Rob: Thank you, Maury. I've always admired you for having had only one love in your life, for forty years, and how you coped with your grief when she died last year. I know you still "talk" to her and that you'll probably never make love to another woman. You are a decent man who treats everyone well. I can't understand why you're here in the group.

Maury: I began seeing Walter two years ago. I realized I was letting my patients take advantage of my good nature and I was undercharging them. And I was letting my office girls tell me what to do. Since seeing Walter, I stopped letting patients use me, have increased my fees and collections and have taken charge of my office. I still have a long way to go in being more assertive. Walter thinks I need to tell him off before I leave.

Mary: Can't you see how smug and arrogant Dr. Turke can be at times? He's just like my father, then. Just like my first husband was, too.

Melissa: And like your second husband is, too!

Mary: Yes, that's true.

John—medical student: Maury, how do you explain having been so lacking in self-assertion?

Maury: After my father died, when I was very young, I had to take care of my sick and bossy mother. I married shortly after Mother died. My wife was just like her. I let her be the boss and we got along well that way. It would have been miserable if I had stood up to her. I could have used some of Walter's arrogance at times, though.

Dr. Turke: I would like to poll the group members if they feel that I am smug and arrogant.

All the people in the group raise their hands.

Rich: The medical students didn't vote! Aren't they allowed to?

Dr. Turke: Of course they may vote.

Both students raise their hands.

Dr. Turke: Is there anyone in the group who is smug and arrogant, at times, as you feel I am?

The group members and students shake their heads no.

Dr. Turke: It might be well to share with you that an ongoing poll of my patients through the years confirms your perception. I plead guilty.

The group nods approvingly to each other.

Dr. Turke: Rich, why are people smug and arrogant in the first place?

Rich: Low self-esteem, I guess.

Dr. Turke: Yes, that's absolutely right. We have now learned that being smug and arrogant may be a compensation for feeling inferior. Isn't it interesting then that I am treating the members of this group for low self-esteem when my self-esteem could, conceivably, be lower than yours.?

The group laughs approvingly.

Mary: You're okay, Turke.

Jean—medical student: Turke?

Mary: I feel very affectionate to Dr. Turke right now. He's a "mensch" and very human. I wanted to call him Walter, but wasn't able to (pensive pause). I wish Dr. Turke had been my father. He'd have made a good husband, too!

Maury: I wish Walter had been my mother!

Jean—medical student: Lance, you've been with Dr. Turke the longest of anyone here. Have you ever felt you were falling in love with him?

Lance: (defensively): Doesn't he wish! Absolutely not!

John—medical student: Then why are you always asking for individual sessions in addition to coming to group?

Lance: (blushes): We need to spend more time with Jody. How is your life going, Jody?

Jody: My husband still goes to the bar every night. He hasn't hit me or pulled a knife on me since I have been coming here, but now he calls me "fat ass" in public. The children ask him to spend time with them and ask him to stop drinking, but he ignores them. They are irritable, depressed, and unmanageable and I'm going to have them see a child psychiatrist.

Rich: The group suggested that you contact an attorney to see what would happen financially in terms of alimony and child support if you should get a divorce. Have you done that?

Jody: No.

Rich: Why not?

Jody: I'm afraid to be alone. I can't be on my own. My mother always babied me and did everything for me. My husband is the only man I've ever been with.

Melissa: I suggested getting all your relatives and your husband's together for an intervention. Surprise him as a group. Inform him they care for him and that they have arranged for a bed for him in a substance abuse program. If he objects, the family withdraws from him. Have you thought about doing this?

Jody: I asked them. They're willing to do it, but I'm afraid. I can't do it!

Melissa: And the consequences to your children?

Jody begins to sob heavily. The group waits for her to stop.

Dr. Turke: Perhaps you'll give the intervention further consideration, Jody?

Jody: Okay. (She turns to Mary.) How're things going with you, Mary?

Mary: I've gone back to college. I told my second husband I was not going to be his maid anymore. Informed him that he ought to be able to be nice to my fifteen-year-old daughter. He seems to be trying. I always walk away from relationships when I get angry rather than trying to work them out. I was going to quit the group some time ago because I felt Dr. Turke was not paying enough attention to me, but I worked it out with him by telling him about my anger. He listened and we resolved the problem. So, maybe I can do the same thing with another man if I try and am patient.

Lance: Good for you, Mary.

Rob: I'm proud of you.

Maury: I like you a lot right now. Keep it up.

Bill: I agree, but, Mary, you seem to have a lot of anger toward men. Your dad was mentioned by you rather unfavorably. Your first husband was blamed, too. You don't appear to take any responsibility for the problems. Takes two to make a problem, you know. You really ought to go to church and take your trouble to God. Spirituality is what you need!

Mary: You son-of-a-bitch, male chauvinist pig bastard! I hate you, you self-righteous jerk!

Lance: Come on, Mary, look at yourself as Bill suggested.

Mary begins to cry, which lasts for about five minutes. She composes herself but is angry again.

Mary: Okay, I'm no angel. I just don't want any fucking man telling me what to do! When I get dressed up, I can have any man I want!

Bill: Thanks for listening, Mary. I care about you and didn't say those things to hurt you.

Mary: I know. (Trace of a smile)

Bill: Rich, why haven't you and your wife gotten spiritual counseling? Your marriage really sounds harmful to you. You and your wife avoid each other, hate each other really. She spends thousands of dollars just shopping. Seems likely you're all alone.

Rich: Some minister you are, advising me! Mind your own goddamn business! Your marriage sounds screwed up, too!

Bill: I disagree with you, Rich. You could give your love to your wife and she might forgive you. The children would be proud of both of you and love you even more. Try to see if you can forgive your wife for the pain she has caused you.

The group agrees by nodding.

Rich: I feel like going out and getting drunk right now and getting laid by some actresses I know from the studio!

John—medical student: Running away from emotional pain rather than working it out seems ill-advised, Rich. I thought the purpose of group was to face things rather than avoiding them.

Dr. Turke: It's your choice, Rich. Think about it. Well, our time is almost up for the day. About ten minutes left. We have a new member and we haven't heard from him. How do you think he feels?

Maury: Sorry, Mitch, we were rude. Tell us about what brings you here.

Mitch: I've been very depressed and carry a suicide note in my wallet at all times. I'm in telecommunications and travel a lot in my car. Lots of times I feel like running my car off the road at high speed and just ending it all. Dr. Turke put me on Paxil and

I started feeling better. He felt I needed to do some talking too, so here I am.

Jody: Tell us about yourself.

Mitch: Well, I got married to someone I didn't know very well when I was twenty. We had two children. Four years into the marriage my wife took the children and left without telling me. I was lonely, met a woman my age. She only has sex with me when I give her money. Her children are undisciplined and don't like me. I can't stand being alone.

John—medical student: Are you still having suicidal thoughts, Mitch?

Mitch: No, they're gone now. Here's my suicide note, Dr. Turke. I don't need it any more. I feel safe in this group and believe it will help me . . .

(I tore up the note in front of the group and threw it in the waste basket.)

Dr. Turke: I see time is up for today. See you next week.

Post Script II

In the Spring of '95, I received a mailing from the Iowa athletic department asking if I wished to purchase football tickets. I purchased seven: three for my daughter, Tiffanie; her husband, Don; their daughter (age 6), Lindsey; three for my son, Garrett; his wife, Stacy; and their daughter (also age 6), Shani. The game was to be the Iowa Hawkeyes against the Michigan State Spartans in East Lansing on October 7th. There were well over 75,000 fans in the stadium with a large contingent from Iowa City. We were seated in middle of the Iowa section in the stadium.

I knew that the rest of my family would be wearing Spartan green and white, but I felt that where I went to school was bigger bond than where I hold my faculty appointment. I decided to wear an Iowa Hawkeye hat with Iowa Hawkeye on the sides and back, and white Iowa shoes with gold laces with Tiger Hawks. I wore an M.S.U. College of Human Medicine sweatshirt and an M.S.U. jacket with an Iowa College of Medicine pin and a Tiger Hawk pin.

I knew that I would be seeing my friend, Hayden Fry, again and I was proud of the way he led the Hawkeyes into the stadium and didn't run up the score. I have enjoyed Iowa cruises with him and am looking forward to the next cruise to the Mexican Riviera. Iowa controlled the ball with a great running game and the defense controlled both sides of the ball. Final score: Iowa–21, M.S.U.–7. Iowa moved into the Top 25 teams in the country. Two brilliant coaches had done their very best and on this day Hayden prevailed. I shed a tear for M.S.U. The grandchildren loved it!

Appendixes

Appendix A

Curriculum Vitae, Walter Turke, M.D., L.F.A.P.A.

MICHIGAN STATE UNIVERSITY

WALTER TURKE, M.D., L.F.A.P.A.
College of Human Medicine
Michigan State University, Saginaw Campus
1000 Houghton Avenue, Saginaw, Michigan 48602
(517) 771-6863

PROFESSIONAL INTERESTS
Teaching Psychiatry to Resident Physicians and Medical Students
Individual and Group Psychotherapy; Psychodynamically-Informed Psychopharmacology

EDUCATIONAL

1948	Academic Diploma, Franklin K. Lane High School, Brooklyn, New York
1952	B.A. Degree, State University of Iowa, Iowa City
1956	M.D. Degree, State University of Iowa, Iowa City
1956-1957	Rotating Internship, Broadlawns County Hospital, Des Moines, Iowa
1957-1958	Resident in Psychiatry, Norwich State Hospital, Connecticut (Personal supervision by faculty from Yale University and the Institute of Living)
1958-1960	Resident in Psychiatry, Mental Health Institute, Cherokee, Iowa, (Personal supervision in psychotherapy in analytically oriented expressive-supportive psychotherapy by former faculty members from Menninger School of Psychiatry), affiliated with University of Iowa and University of Nebraska.
May, 1974	Laboratory of Community Psychiatry, Harvard Medical School with Gerald Caplan, M.D.
1975-1980	Postgraduate Courses in Psychiatry, University of Michigan Medical Center, Ann Arbor, Michigan

ACHIEVEMENTS

1957	Diplomate, National Board of Medical Examiners
1963	Diplomate, American Board of Psychiatry and Neurology (P)
1974	Fellow, American Psychiatric Association
1993	Life Fellow, American Psychiatric Association
1993 & 1994	Excellence in Clinical Teaching Award, College of Human Medicine, Michigan State University, Minority Medical Student Association
1995	Excellence in Teaching Award, College of Human Medicine, Michigan State University, Class of 1995; Certificate of Appreciation, CHM/MSU Minority Medial Student Association

COLLEGE OF
HUMAN MEDICINE
Office of the Assistant Dean
for Saginaw
Saginaw Cooperative
Hospitals, Inc.
1000 Houghton Avenue
Suite 1000
Saginaw, Michigan
48602
517/771-6878
FAX: 517/753-3439

ACTIVE MEDICAL LICENSURE
Michigan (#30058)

MEMBERSHIPS
Association of Directors of Medical Student Education in Psychiatry
Association for Academic Psychiatry
Michigan Psychiatric Society
American Psychiatric Association
World Psychiatric Association
American Medical Association
Michigan State Medical Society
Saginaw County Medical Society

CURRENT PROFESSIONAL ACTIVITIES

July, 1988- Clinical Professor (promoted 1/17/95), Department of Psychiatry, College of Human Medicine, Michigan State University, East Lansing, Michigan; Psychiatry Clerkship Coordinator, College of Human Medicine, Michigan State University, Saginaw Campus; Member, Medical Student Education Committee, Department of Psychiatry, CHM/MSU; Member, Prematriculation Programs Subsidiary Committee of MSU College of Human Medicine Curriculum Committee

July, 1988- Director of Psychiatry Department, Saginaw Cooperative Hospitals, Inc. (a medical education corporation and the Saginaw Campus of Michigan State University); Member of the following SCHI Committees: Academic Affairs, Program Directors, Ethics, Spirituality and Human Values in Medicine, and Continuing Medical Education; also a member of the Ethics Committee for the Saginaw County Medical Society

EXPERIENCE HIGHLIGHTS

1989-1991.... Clinical Director of Outpatient Services, St. Luke's Health Center, Saginaw, Michigan

Associate Professor, Department of Psychiatry, College of Human Medicine, Michigan State University, East Lansing, Michigan

Psychiatry Clerkship Coordinator, College of Human Medicine, Michigan State University, Saginaw Campus (Developed new psychiatry clerkship teaching site(s) for MSU medical students on the Saginaw Campus.)

1986-1988.... Medical Director, Psychiatry, Bay Medical Center, Bay City, Michigan (28 bed teaching and training unit for Michigan State University medical students)

Associate Professor, Department of Psychiatry, College of Human Medicine, Michigan State University, East Lansing, Michigan

Psychiatry Clerkship Coordinator, College of Human Medicine, Michigan State University, Saginaw Campus

1985-1986.... Assistant Professor, Department of Psychiatry, School of Medicine, University of South Dakota

Medical Director, McKennan Hospital Mental Health Inpatient Unit, Sioux Falls, South Dakota (49 bed teaching and training unit for Department of Psychiatry)

Appointed Program Director of University of South Dakota Psychiatry Residency Program (had decided to return to Michigan and Michigan State University)

1982-1985.... Psychotherapy Supervisor, Residency Training Program, Department of Psychiatry and Consultant Outpatient Section, Maricopa Medical Center, Phoenix, Arizona

Lecturer and Clinical Associate, University of Arizona, College of Medicine

Board Member, Arizona Group Psychotherapy Society

Vice President, Phoenix Psychiatric Council and Member, Executive Committee, Arizona Psychiatric Society

Part-time Private Practice, Scottsdale, Arizona; Staff, Scottsdale Camelback Hospital. Treatment of N.F.L. players referred for substance abuse problems in Scottsdale Camelback Hospital.

1975-1981.... Private Practice, Traverse City, Michigan

Assistant Clinical Professor, Department of Psychiatry, CHM/MSU

1971-1975.... Clinical Director and Director of Community Health Division, Traverse City State Hospital, Traverse City, Michigan

Assistant Clinical Professor, Department of Psychiatry, CHM/MSU

1962-1971.... Private Practice, Woodland Hills, Los Angeles, CA Outpatient psychodynamic psychotherapy (individual and group), largely with patients from entertainment industry.

1960-1962.... Lt. Commander, Medical Corps, Neuropsychiatry Section, U.S. Naval Hospital, Portsmouth, Virginia. (In charge of hospitalized officers and directed the outpatient clinic.)

CONSULTING ACTIVITIES

Aleda E. Lutz Veterans Affairs Medical Center, Saginaw, Michigan
Catholic Family Services, Saginaw, Michigan
Norman Westlund Child Guidance Clinic, Saginaw, Michigan

RESEARCH AND TEACHING INTERESTS

Teaching medical students to recognize "core conflictural relationship themes" in their patients; precise measurement scales* for each technique make it easy to evaluate the therapist's performance.

*Luborsky, Lester, Principles of Psychoanalytic Psychotherapy, Basic Books, New York, 1984

Will set up protocol as soon as we can recruit more psychiatrists to come to Saginaw.

PAPERS WRITTEN FOR TEACHING PURPOSES (10/85 - 3/93)

"Management of Major Depression for the Primary Physician" (Published in the South Dakota State Medical Journal, May 1986)

"Teaching Psychiatry to Medical Students in Outpatient Settings in Rural Areas (Presented at Annual Meeting of Association of Directors of Medical Student Education in Psychiatry, June 12, 1993, and at Annual Meeting of Association for Academic Psychiatry, March 12, 1993.)

"Period of Transition in a Michigan State Hospital - Parts I & II"

"Plan for Reorganization of Arizona State Hospital"

"Psychotherapeutic Interventions in Schizophrenia"

"Karen: Psychotherapeutic Intervention in Schizophrenia"

"Management of the Schizophrenia Outpatient for the Primary Physician"

"A Case of AIDS"

"Starry, Starry Night - A Birthday Tribute to Vincent VanGogh from His' Friend, Walter"

"Papua New Guinea Odyssey"

Appendix B

University of Iowa Letter—President's Club 10/19/93

THE UNIVERSITY OF IOWA

October 19, 1993

Walter Turke, MD, LFAPA

Dear Dr. Turke:

It is a great pleasure to welcome you to membership in the Presidents Club. My colleagues and I are deeply grateful for the generous support which qualifies you for this membership. The University is in an exciting and invigorating era of change and advancement in which you can take pride.

I look forward to seeing you at the special events hosted by the Presidents Club in the months and years ahead.

Yours sincerely,

Hunter R. Rawlings III
President

Office of the President 101 Jessup Hall Iowa City, Iowa 52242-1316 319/335-3549

MICHIGAN STATE
UNIVERSITY

February 7, 1995

Walter Turke, M.D.
1000 Houghton
Suite 1000
Saginaw, MI 48602

Dear Dr. Turke:

I am delighted to inform you that the Department of Psychiatry has approved your promotion to Clinical Professor. The appropriate paperwork is being processed and you should receive official notification shortly.

It is a pleasure for me to personally congratulate you and at the same time thank you again for your contributions to the Department and to our medical students.

Sincerely,

Norbert B. Enzer, M.D.
Professor and Chairperson
/k

c: William Abbett, Ph.D., Dean, College of Human Medicine
David Engstrom, M.D., Assistant Dean, Saginaw Campus
James R. Springer, Ed.D., Director, Medical Student Programs in Psychiatry

DEPARTMENT OF
PSYCHIATRY
COLLEGES OF
HUMAN MEDICINE AND OSTEOPATHIC MEDICINE
East Fee Hall
East Lansing, Michigan
48824-1316
FAX: 517 / 336-2893

Michigan State University

College of Human Medicine

This is to Certify that

Walter Turke, M.D.

has been appointed

Clinical Professor

in the

Department Psychiatry

1995

Dean

Assistant Dean

Chairperson

Appendix C

MSU College of Human Medicine Dean's Letter 12/28/93

MICHIGAN STATE
UNIVERSITY

December 28, 1993

Walter Turke, M.D.

Bay City, Michigan 48706

Dear Dr. Turke:

I am writing to express my sincerest appreciation for your recent contribution of $1,000 to the College of Human Medicine. At your special request, this gift will be directed to the Women's Scholarship Fund.

I know I need not tell you how vitally important private support is to the future of this College. In these times of heightened fiscal austerity and impending healthcare reform, it is clear that charitable support coupled with thoughtful foresight and vision will be increasingly pivotal to sustaining the standard of excellence we have come to expect in medical education, research and training. Through your support, you tangibly have reaffirmed your commitment to the College and its mission. I cannot help but believe that your generosity will serve as a powerful example for others -- particularly alumni and your faculty peers -- to also give.

Your leadership is evidenced not only by your valued service as a distinguished member of this faculty; it also is clearly demonstrated through your generous philanthropic support. For this, I thank you. Your many contributions to the College are indeed exemplary.

Sincerely,

William S. Abbett, Ph.D.
Dean

COLLEGE OF
HUMAN MEDICINE
Office of the Dean
East Fee Hall
East Lansing, Michigan
48824-1316
517/353-1730
FAX: 517/355-0342

Appendix D
Prematriculation Committee Letter 5/19/94

MICHIGAN STATE
UNIVERSITY

May 19, 1994

Walter

Dear ~~Prematriculation~~ Committee Member:

A short note of thanks and appreciation for your time and effort during the past year. All in all, I believe we accomplished a great deal. Although the A.B.L.E. program was well established and an ongoing success, review and fine tuning will always be necessary. Our greatest task was the Medical Scholars Program and we <u>did</u> accomplish a great deal. The articulation of goals and objectives was a difficult task, but we did it. In addition, a flexible but rational curriculum has been proposed. Now we await the will of the Curriculum Committee. No feedback at this writing.

Once again, thank you so very much for all your effort and help.

Very truly yours,

Larry

Lawrence M. Ross. M.D., Ph.D
Chairperson

LMR/ld

COLLEGE OF
HUMAN MEDICINE

Office of Academic Programs

A-254 Life Sciences Building
East Lansing, Michigan
48824-1317

517/353-5440
FAX: 517/336-1051

Appendix E

American Psychiatric Association, Life Fellow

American Psychiatric Association

Be it known to all by these presents that on the recommendation of the Committee on Membership and the approval of the Board of Trustees this Association has elected

Walter Turke, M.D.

to be a

Life Fellow

in recognition of significant contributions to Psychiatry.

Witness the hand of the President and the Secretary and the seal of the Association this first day of January, 1993.

President

Secretary

American Psychiatric Association, Fellow Certificate

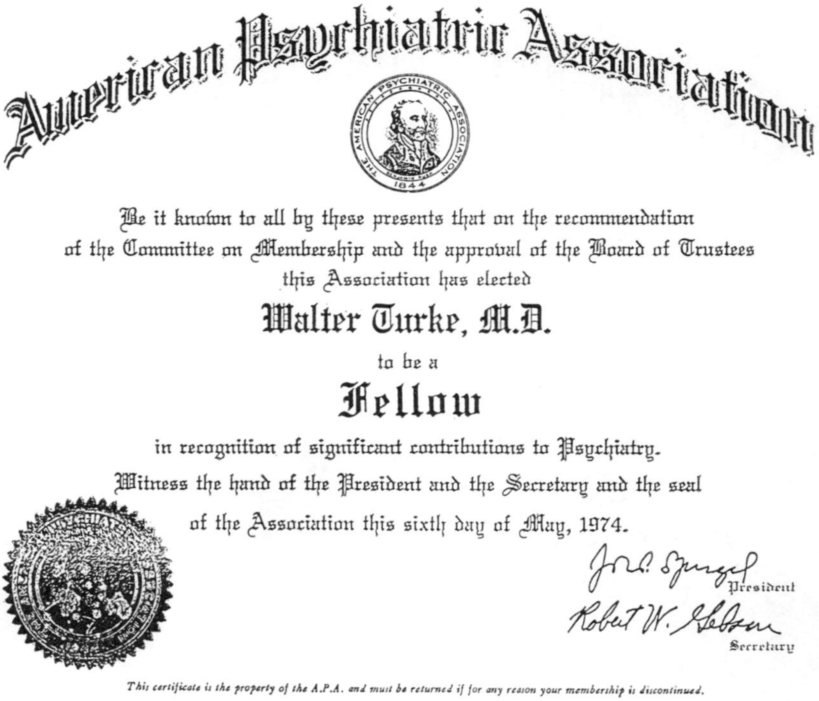

American Psychiatric Association

Be it known to all by these presents that on the recommendation of the Committee on Membership and the approval of the Board of Trustees this Association has elected

Walter Turke, M.D.

to be a

Fellow

in recognition of significant contributions to Psychiatry.

Witness the hand of the President and the Secretary and the seal of the Association this sixth day of May, 1974.

President

Robert W. Gibson

Secretary

This certificate is the property of the A.P.A. and must be returned if for any reason your membership is discontinued.

Michigan State Board of Registration in Medicine, License

Department of Licensing and Regulation

Michigan State Board of Registration in Medicine

Lansing — CIRCUMSPICE — Michigan

Know all men by these presents that

Walter Turke

is a duly licensed

Physician and Surgeon

in accordance with the "Medical Practice Act No. 237, Public Act 1899 as amended" of the State of Michigan, and is authorized to practice medicine and surgery in all their branches in this state.

In witness whereof, we have hereunto fixed our hands and the seal of the Board this twenty-first day of June, 1971.

No. 30058

[illegible], M. D.
President of the Board

John M. Wellman, M. D.
Secretary of the Board

American Board of Psychiatry and Neurology, Certificate

The American Board of Psychiatry and Neurology

Incorporated 1934

This is to certify that

Walter Turke, M.D.

has satisfied the requirements of the Board
and is hereby certified as qualified to practice the specialty of

Psychiatry

Certificate No. 7813

A.B. Baker
President

Hugh T. Carmichael
Vice President

Ewald W. Busse
Secretary

April, 1963

National Board of Medical Examiners, Certificate

National Board of Medical Examiners
of the
United States of America

Walter Turke, M.D.

having satisfied all the requirements and having successfully passed the examinations is hereby declared a

Diplomate of the National Board of Medical Examiners

Attest [signature]
President of the Board

Philadelphia, Pa. July 1 1957

[signature]
Executive Secretary of the Board

Certificate No. 35447

State University of Iowa, Degree

State University of Iowa

ON RECOMMENDATION OF THE FACULTY OF THE

COLLEGE OF MEDICINE

AND UNDER THE AUTHORITY OF THE STATUTES OF IOWA
AND THE STATE BOARD OF REGENTS

THE STATE UNIVERSITY OF IOWA HAS CONFERRED THE DEGREE OF

DOCTOR OF MEDICINE

UPON

WALTER TURKE

WHO HAS HONORABLY FULFILLED ALL OF THE REQUIREMENTS PRESCRIBED BY THE UNIVERSITY FOR THIS DEGREE

WITNESS THE SEAL OF THE UNIVERSITY AND THE SIGNATURES OF DULY AUTHORIZED OFFICERS GIVEN AT IOWA CITY ON THE EIGHTH DAY OF JUNE IN THE YEAR OF OUR LORD ONE THOUSAND NINE HUNDRED AND FIFTY SIX

Dwight Rider
PRESIDENT, STATE BOARD OF REGENTS

Virgil M. Hancher
PRESIDENT OF THE UNIVERSITY

Norman B. Nelson
DEAN

Appendix F

Introductory Memo to MSU Medical Students 6/17/94

MICHIGAN STATE
UNIVERSITY

MEMORANDUM

TO: Angie Domingo, MSU III — Dominic Maxwell, MSU III
Karen Jorgensen, MSU III — Thomas Ronay, MSU III
James Lieber, MSU III — Allison Schwanda, MSU III

FROM: Walter Turke, M.D., L.F.A.P.A. WT
Associate Professor, Department of Psychiatry
Psychiatry Clerkship Coordinator, Saginaw Campus
College of Human Medicine, Michigan State University

DATE: June 17, 1994

SUBJ: PSYCHIATRY CLERKSHIP (PSC 608)
Saginaw Cooperative Hospitals, Inc.
June 27 through August 19, 1994

Welcome! The Department of Psychiatry of Michigan State University is biopsychosocial in orientation. This clerkship is designed to expose medical students to the contemporary practice of psychiatry. It is my intention to make the clerkship enjoyable as well as a potential growth experience. The Medical Student Education Committee (of which I am a member) of the Department of Psychiatry has made the curriculum arduous.

I will coordinate your adult outpatient experience in group therapy, individual psychodynamic psychotherapy and psychodynamically-informed psychopharmacology at the SCHI/MSU Psychiatry Practice Center and at the V.A.M.C. Center for Counseling. Inpatient experience will be obtained at HealthSource Saginaw (formerly known as Saginaw Community Hospital) White Pine Psychiatric Center under the direction of Harold Lenhart, M.D., Assistant Clinical Professor. Geriatric and Substance Abuse patient experience will be coordinated by Andrew Lovy, D.O. , Clinical Professor, at White Pine Psychiatric Center. Kaushik J. Raval, M.D., (whose faculty appointment is pending), will provide consultation-liaison psychiatry at Veterans Administration Medical Center and additional adult outpatient experience at the VAMC Center for Counseling. Denise Dutchak, M.D., Clinical Instructor, will provide Child and Adolescent Psychiatry at the Bay City A.C.T. Program, Michigan Psych Associates, Delta Family Clinic, and W.P.P.C.

COLLEGE OF HUMAN MEDICINE
Serving the People
MICHIGAN STATE UNIVERSITY

COLLEGE OF
HUMAN MEDICINE
Office of the Assistant Dean for Saginaw
Saginaw Cooperative Hospitals, Inc.
1000 Houghton Avenue
Suite 1000
Saginaw, Michigan
48602
517/771-6878
FAX: 517/753-3439

REMEMBER TO ALWAYS WEAR YOUR WHITE COATS WITH I.D. TAGS AT ALL CLERKSHIP SITES.

Attendance is required for all activities listed on the daily Psychiatry Clerkship Schedule. (A draft of the schedule is enclosed.) Absence without notification is considered unprofessional behavior. If you are unable to attend a required lecture/activity, it is your responsibility to notify the lecturer/preceptor and me, or my Administrative Assistant, if I am unavailable. You will be informed of any changes in the daily schedule.

(Continue on next page...)

MEMORANDUM
June 17, 1994
Page Two

We will have Clinical Seminars in two-hour time slots covering the nosology, psychopathology, psychodynamics, psychopharmacology and psychotherapy of the subject matter, i.e., Schizophrenia, for example. We will cover the same material that was formerly presented in lecture format. Prior to the seminars, students must read the basic texts:

**Psychiatry: Diagnosis & Therapy, A Lange Clinical Manual, Second Edition, JA Flaherty, JM Davis, PG Janicak;
**Depression in Primary Care: Detection, Diagnosis, and Treatment, U.S. Department of Health and Human Services, April 1993;
**DSM-IV Draft Criteria, A.P.A.;
**DSM-III-R Casebook;
Behavior and Medicine, D Wedding;
Introductory Textbook of Psychiatry, NC Andreasen and DW Black.

(**TEXTS CAN BE CHECKED OUT FROM MY OFFICE FOR YOUR USE DURING THE CLERKSHIP. YOU DO NOT HAVE TO PURCHASE THEM--the other texts were previously used in pre-clinical courses.)

It is also expected that you have retained the information learned during Block II, i.e., the Introductory Textbook of Psychiatry, and Behavior and Medicine. In addition to reviewing the required texts, you might read the American Journal of Psychiatry, Psychiatric Annals, The Harvard Mental Health Letter, and Behavioral Science for Medical Students, FS Sierles, all of which may be found in my office.

A new teaching format for psychopharmacology has also been implemented per student request. Students will make out 3 X 5 cards on the patients they see. The information will cover the essentials of the drug they have prescribed for the patient, including mode of action, time of onset, side effects, etc. These will be presented to the group whenever there are 20 minute breaks during the Psychodynamically-Informed Psychopharmacology Clinic.

The faculty will be your role models. We will do what we want you to do. We will explain to you why we did what we did. We will ask you challenging questions which will be high-level questions. You will become actively involved in appropriate practice. We will provide constructive feedback so that you will know what you are doing. We will share the following with you: (1) what was done correctly, (2) what was done incorrectly, and (3) what should work in the future.

We have expanded the evening Psychiatry Club to invite all medical students on the Saginaw Campus, which will be held every other week during the clerkship. We will meet at my condo for Pizza, Pepsi and for informal discussions and camaraderie from 6:00 to 9:00 P.M. We usually watch a video such as, "What About Bob!", "The Boys in the Band", "The Music Lovers" (the life of Pytor Illyich Tchaikovsky), or Spike Lee's "Jungle Fever". Possible diagnoses and psychodynamics are then discussed.

(Continue on next page...)

Students' attention is invited to the Psychiatry Clerkship Log Book which summarizes the objectives and additional requirements for the clerkship. Drs. Lenhart, Lovy, and I have divided up the topics to be covered. Sign off for completion will be done by the faculty professor teaching that material. The expectation is that all students will complete 100% of the objectives (as presented in the Log Book). If you chose, you may pick up the other clerkship materials and books prior to starting the clerkship.

On MONDAY, JUNE 27, at 8:00 A.M. all students are to meet in my MSU/SCHI office which is located in the basement of the Saginaw Medical Center (see enclosed map). We will have a group picture taken for the Department of Psychiatry wall, so wear your white jackets. Also, a 25-item, multiple choice pre-test will be administered to all medical students. The results of the pre-test are not included in any evaluation. It is used to provide students with some assessment of their knowledge in the content areas of psychiatry, familiarize them with the format of the final examination and to provide a baseline by which to measure improvement over the course of the clerkship. The test will be reviewed with you afterwards unlike the final examination which is a restricted test and will not be discussed with you. You must get 70% to pass Psychiatry and at least 80% to be considered for Honors.

If you fail the final examination, you will receive a CP grade. If you pass the re-take exam, your grade will be logged as CP-P. If you fail the second exam, remediation is required and you will have to meet with me to discuss this. If you become ill and cannot complete the clerkship, your grade will be logged as ET (extension).

Prior to taking the final exam, please turn in all clerkship materials and complete the clerkship evaluation forms. Remember that we value your opinions and suggestions and will be responsive to them in planning the next clerkships. My Administrative Assistant will hold them in strictest confidence until the grades are in and the Dean's letters written. The Department of Psychiatry directives stipulate that all students are required to write six questions to be used on future Psychiatry Clerkship exams: one extended matching, one mini case study, and the other questions may be R-type, mini case study, or traditional multiple choice. The choices for answers need to be from five options. It is not necessary to provide a reference for these questions, however, the correct answer needs to be identified. The Department asks that you do not use "true or false" questions. These need to be handed in prior to the final examination with your clinical case write-up with psychodynamic formulation.

If any students are interested in joining a Gay/Lesbian Support Group, please let me know so you can be included.

(Continue on next page...)

During this clerkship, I would appreciate your attempting to avoid the following:

"Nervous"	-Please use the term "anxious".
"Upset"	-Rather "I am angry" or "I am afraid".
"Bad feelings"	-There are no "bad feelings" -- only human ones; we are responsible for our actions.
"Foul language"	-I would prefer you to use quotes to describe the patient's expletives as they may give a clue to the psychodynamics. However, if you are not comfortable with this, please use the term "street language".
"It is very sad"	-Frequently used perjuratively in our culture meaning "bad".
"O.K."	-Please refrain from use when interviewing; may be construed as judgmental by the patient and demonstrates anxiety in the interviewer.

I would also like to give you some things to think about. Is it possible that at times love + fear = hate; joy + fear = guilt; pleasure + guilt = disgust??

Please remember there are at least three things troubling each of your patients:

1. Lack of love -The "cure" for this is to offer the patient respect.

2. Anxiety -The "cure" is communication--the patient talks and we listen (you may grow a "third ear" on this clerkship!).

3. Guilt -The "cure" is understanding.

Please report any problems or concerns to me promptly. If you have any questions, please feel free to contact me for information and help. I can be reached via my Administrative Assistant, Kim Betzold, at 771-6863. My door is always open to you...

cc: David Engstrom, M.D.
Denise Dutchak, M.D.
Harold Lenhart, M.D.
Andrew Lovy, D.O.
Kaushik Raval, M.D.
James Springer, Ed.D.
Barbara Sucher, M.B.A.

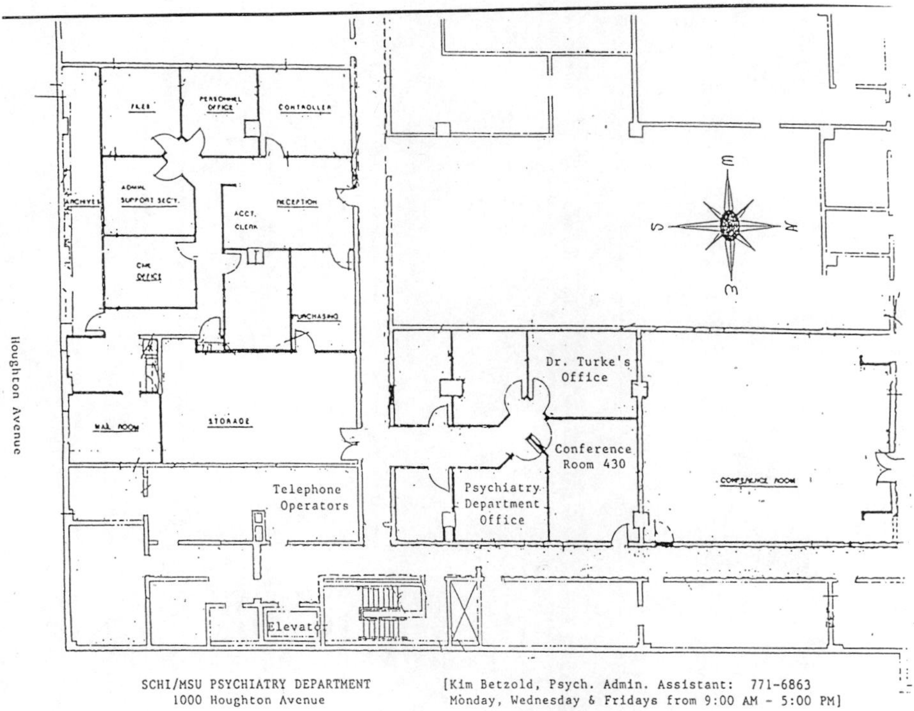

SCHI/MSU PSYCHIATRY DEPARTMENT
1000 Houghton Avenue

(Southeast corner of the basement of the Saginaw Medical Center.)

[Kim Betzold, Psych. Admin. Assistant: 771-6863
Monday, Wednesday & Fridays from 9:00 AM - 5:00 PM]

BASEMENT PLAN

Clerkship Schedule

MICHIGAN STATE UNIVERSITY * SAGINAW COOPERATIVE HOSPITALS, INC.

PSYCHIATRY CLERKSHIP REQUIRED SCHEDULE, SAGINAW CAMPUS

SUMMER II TERM 1994

SCHI - Dr. Turke's Office 771-6863
VAMC - Counseling Center 791-2242 or 793-2340, ex. 3730
CMH - Community Mental Health w/Dr.Lenhart 797-3400
SGH - Saginaw General Hospital M.H.U. 771-4250

WPPC - White Pine Psychiatric Center 790-7736
Dr. Lenhart's Private Practice Office 793-5303
Dr. Lovy's Office 790-7734
Dr. Vasilenko's Office 771-6839

MONDAY, JUNE 27	TUESDAY, JUNE 28	WEDNESDAY, JUNE 29	THURSDAY, JUNE 30	FRIDAY, JULY 1
8:00 - 12:00 Noon "Orientation to Psychiatry & Pre-Test" Walter Turke, M.D. SCHI/MSU Office	8:30 - 10:00 A.M. Clinical Seminar: "Psychodynamics of Psychoactive Substance Use Disorders & Eating Disorders" Walter Turke, M.D. SCHI/MSU Office	7:30 - 11:00 A.M. VAMC Counseling Center w/Dr.Turke [Practice Exp]	8:00 - 12:00 Noon WPPC w/Dr.Lovy Students A,B,C	8:30 - 10:30 A.M. "Organic Mental Disorders" Jan Caputo, Ph.D., Psy.D. Saginaw Medical Center Lower Level, Room 430
	10:30 - 12:30 P.M. Sleep & Pain Disorders w/Dr.Chatfield SLH South Campus 515 N.Michigan Ave. (758-2823)		8:00 - 11:30 A.M. VAMC w/Dr.Raval Students D,E,F	
1:00 - 3:00 P.M. Clinical Seminar: "Psychodynamics" Walter Turke, M.D. SCHI/MSU Office	1:00 - 5:00 P.M. "Orientation to WPPC" Joe Rainey, ACSW & Staff	1:00 - 5:00 P.M. "Orientation to VAMC" and Consultation Liaison Psych w/Kaushik Raval, M.D. VAMC Counseling Center	1:00 - 5:00 P.M. Independent Study Students D,E,F	1:00 - 5:00 P.M. Independent Study All Students
3:00 - 4:30 P.M. SCHI/MSU Group Therapy w/Dr.Turke Students D,E,F	6:00 - 9:00 P.M. PSYCHIATRY CLUB "Memories of Hollywood" with video Dr.Turke's condo		1:30 - 4:00 P.M. Psychodynamically Informed Psychopharm. Clinic w/Dr.Turke and	
3:00 - 5:00 P.M. Independent Study Students A,B,C			5:00 - 6:30 P.M. SCHI/MSU Group Therapy w/Dr.Turke Students A,B,C	

*********************** [DR.LENHART IS ON VACATION FROM JUNE 27 THROUGH JULY 4] ***********************

*** [DR.TURKE IS ON VACATION TODAY] ***

**PLEASE NOTE: Topics of discussions to take place in the event of "no shows":
"Neuropsychiatry of A.I.D.S.", "Vincent Van Gogh—His Life & His Times"
"Medication Compliance: Transference, Counter-Transference & Resistance"
"Loneliness, Intimacy & Hostility", "Death and Dying", "Depression in the Elderly"

TUESDAYS: Dr.Turke is at Westlund Child Guidance Clinic from 7:00-8:30 AM.

FRIDAYS: Dr.Turke is at Catholic Family Services from 7:00-10:00 AM on 5/6, 5/20, 6/10, 6/24.

Student A-Angie Domingo, MSU III
Student B-Karen Jorgensen, MSU III
Student C-James Lieber, MSU III
Student D-Dominic Maxwell, MSU III
Student E-Thomas Ronay, MSU III
Student F-Allison Schwanda, MSU III

MSU/SCHI PSYCHIATRY CLERKSHIP REQUIRED SCHEDULE
SUMMER II TERM 1994
PAGE 2

SCHI - Dr. Turke's Office 771-6863
VAMC - Counseling Center 791-2242 or 793-2340, ex. 3730
CMH - Community Mental Health w/Dr.Lenhart 797-3400
SGH - Saginaw General Hospital M.H.U. 771-4250
WPPC - White Pine Psychiatric Center 790-7736
Dr. Lenhart's Private Practice Office 793-5303
Dr. Lovy's Office 790-7734

MONDAY, JULY 4	TUESDAY, JULY 5	WEDNESDAY, JULY 6	THURSDAY, JULY 7	FRIDAY, JULY 8
	8:30 - 10:00 A.M. Clinical Seminar: "Paraphilias and Sexual Dysfunctions" Walter Turke, M.D. SCHI/MSU Office	7:30 - 11:00 A.M. VAMC Counseling Center w/Dr.Turke [Practice Exp]	8:00 - 12:00 Noon WPPC w/Dr.Lenhart Students D,E,F	8:00 - 12:00 Noon WPPC w/Dr.Lenhart Students D,E,F
	10:30 - 12:30 P.M. Sleep & Pain Disorders w/Dr.Chatfield SLH South Campus 515 N.Michigan Ave. (758-2823)		8:00 - 12:00 Noon SCHI/MSU Psychiatry Practice Ctr. W/Dr.Turke Students A,B,C	8:00 - 12:00 Noon VAMC Counseling Center w/Dr.Raval Students A,B,C
********* HOLIDAY **********	1:00 - 5:00 P.M. Community Mental Health w/Dr.Lenhart Students D & E	12:00 - 5:00 P.M. A.C.T. Program-Saginaw w/Dr.Lenhart Students D & E	1:00 - 5:00 P.M. Community Mental Health w/Dr.Lenhart Students D & E	2:00 - 4:00 P.M. Clinical Seminar: "Adjustment Disorders", "Crisis Intervention", "Marital Therapy", "Separations", and "Sexual Therapy" Walter Turke, M.D. SCHI/MSU Office
	1:00 - 5:00 P.M. WPPC/Pt.Evaluations Students A,B,C	12:30 - 2:30 P.M. VietNam Vets PTSD Group w/Chaplain A.Todd and William Koruna, MSW VAMC Counseling Center Student F	1:00 - 5:00 P.M. VAMC Counseling Center w/Dr.Raval Student F	
	1:00 - 5:00 P.M. VAMC Counseling Center w/Dr.Raval Student F	1:00 - 5:00 P.M. Consultation Liaison Psych w/Kaushik Raval, M.D. VAMC Counseling Center Students A,B,C	1:00 - 5:00 P.M. Psychodynamically Informed Psychopharm. Clinic w/Dr.Turke and 5:00 - 6:30 P.M. SCHI/MSU Group Therapy w/Dr.Turke Students A,B,C	
			****** [DR.LOVY IS ATTENDING A CONFERENCE FROM JULY 7 THROUGH JULY 9] ********	

Student A-Angie Domingo, MSU III
Student B-Karen Jorgensen, MSU III
Student C-James Lieber, MSU III
Student D-Dominic Maxwell, MSU III
Student E-Thomas Ronay, MSU III
Student F-Allison Schwanda, MSU III

MSU/SCHI PSYCHIATRY CLERKSHIP REQUIRED SCHEDULE
SUMMER II TERM 1994
PAGE 3

SCHI - Dr. Turke's Office 771-6863
VAMC - Counseling Center 791-2242 or 793-2340, ex. 3730
CMH - Community Mental Health w/Dr.Lenhart 797-3400
SGH - Saginaw General Hospital M.H.U. 771-4250
WPPC - White Pine Psychiatric Center 790-7736
Dr. Lenhart's Private Practice Office 793-5303
Dr. Lovy's Office 790-7734

MONDAY, JULY 11	TUESDAY, JULY 12	WEDNESDAY, JULY 13	THURSDAY, JULY 14	FRIDAY, JULY 15
8:00 - 12:00 Noon WPPC InPt. W/Dr.Lenhart Students D & E	8:30 - 10:30 A.M. Clinical Seminar: "Schizophrenia and Paranoid Disorders" Walter Turke, M.D. SCHI/MSU Office	7:30 - 10:00 A.M. VAMC Counseling Center w/Dr.Turke [Practice Exp]	8:00 - 12:00 Noon WPPC w/Dr.Lenhart Students D,E,F	8:00 - 12:00 Noon WPPC w/Dr.Lenhart Students D,E,F
8:00 - 12:00 Noon Psych In-Takes w/Dr.Raval VAMC Counseling Center Students A,B,C	10:30 - 12:30 P.M. "Psychopharmacology of Affective Disorders and Anti-psychotics" G.Robert DeYoung, Pharm D Saginaw Medical Center Lower Level, Room 430		8:00 - 12:00 Noon WPPC w/Dr.Lovy Students A,B,C	8:00 - 12:00 Noon WPPC w/Dr.Lovy Students A,B,C
8:00 - 12:00 Noon Delta Family Clinic w/Dr.Dutchak (684-9313) Student F				
1:00 - 3:00 P.M. SCHI/MSU Psychiatry Practice Center w/DrTurke and	1:00 - 5:00 P.M. Community Mental Health w/Dr.Lenhart Students D & F	12:00 - 5:00 P.M. A.C.T. Program-Bay City w/Dr.Dutchak Student D	1:00 - 5:00 P.M. Community Mental Health w/Dr.Lenhart Students D & F	1:00 - 2:00 P.M. "Physical Intervention" Randy Lobdell, CTRS SGH/MHU Activity Room
3:00 - 4:30 P.M. SCHI/MSU Group Therapy w/Dr.Turke Students D,E,F	1:00 - 5:00 P.M. WPPC/Pt.Evaluations Students A,B,C	12:00 - 5:00 P.M. A.C.T. Program-Saginaw w/Dr.Lenhart Students E & F	1:30 - 5:00 P.M. Michigan Psych Assoc. w/Dr.Dutchak (895-2375) Student E	2:30 - 3:30 P.M. "Spirituality in Medicine" Rev.Robert Leas Saginaw Medical Center Lower Level, Room 430
1:00 - 4:00 P.M. WPPC w/Dr.Lovy Students A,B,C	1:00 - 5:00 P.M. VAMC Counseling Center w/Dr.Raval Student E	1:00 - 5:00 P.M. Consultation Liaison Psych w/Kaushik Raval, M.D. VAMC Counseling Center Students A,B,C	1:00 - 5:00 P.M. Psychodynamically Informed Psychopharm. Clinic w/Dr.Turke and	
	6:00 - 9:00 P.M. PSYCHIATRY CLUB Video:"The Sheltering Sky" with Debra Winger and John Malkovich Dr.Turke's condo		5:00 - 6:30 P.M. SCHI/MSU Group Therapy w/Dr.Turke Students A,B,C	* * * [DR.TURKE IS ON VACATION TODAY] * * *

Student A-Angie Domingo, MSU III
Student B-Karen Jorgensen, MSU III
Student C-James Lieber, MSU III
Student D-Dominic Maxwell, MSU III
Student E-Thomas Roney, MSU III
Student F-Allison Schwanda, MSU III

MSU/SCHI PSYCHIATRY CLERKSHIP REQUIRED SCHEDULE
SUMMER II TERM 1994
PAGE 4

SCHI - Dr. Turke's Office 771-6863
VAMC - Counseling Center 791-2242 or 793-2340, ex. 3730
CMH - Community Mental Health w/Dr.Lenhart 797-3400
SGH - Saginaw General Hospital M.H.U. 771-4250
WPPC - White Pine Psychiatric Center 790-7736
Dr. Lenhart's Private Practice Office 793-5303
Dr. Lovy's Office 790-7734

MONDAY, JULY 18	TUESDAY, JULY 19	WEDNESDAY, JULY 20	THURSDAY, JULY 21	FRIDAY, JULY 22
8:00 - 12:00 Noon WPPC InPt. W/Dr.Lenhart Students E & F	8:30 - 10:30 A.M. Clinical Seminar: "Personality Disorders & Somatoform Disorders" Walter Turke, M.D. SCHI/MSU Office	7:30 - 10:30 A.M. VAMC Counseling Center w/Dr.Turke [Practice Exp]	8:00 - 11:45 A.M. WPPC w/Dr.Lenhart Students D,E,F	8:00 - 12:00 Noon WPPC w/Dr.Lenhart Students D,E,F
8:00 - 12:00 Noon Psych In-Takes w/Dr.Raval VAMC Counseling Center Students A,B,C		10:30 - 12:00 P.M. "Introduction to Psychological Testing" Ross Whitman, Ph.D. and Nancy Howkanech, Ph.D. VAMC Counseling Center	8:00 - 11:45 A.M. WPPC w/Dr.Lovy Students A,B,C	8:00 - 12:00 Noon WPPC w/Dr.Lovy Students A,B,C
8:00 - 12:00 Noon Independent Study Student D			12:15 - 1:30 P.M. FAMILY PRACTICE BEHAVIOR SCIENCE LECTURE "Overview of Affective Disorders" W.Turke, M.D. SLH Bickel-Geyer D.R.	
1:00 - 3:00 P.M. SCHI/MSU Psychiatry Practice Center w/DrTurke and	1:00 - 5:00 P.M. Community Mental Health w/Dr.Lenhart Students E & F	12:00 - 5:00 P.M. A.C.T. Program-Saginaw w/Dr.Lenhart Students E & F	1:30 - 5:00 P.M. Community Mental Health w/Dr.Lenhart Students E & F	1:00 - 2:00 P.M. "Pharmaco Therapy in Bipolar Disorders" G.Robert DeYoung, Pharm D Saginaw Medical Center Lower Level, Room 430
3:00 - 4:30 P.M. SCHI/MSU Group Therapy w/Dr.Turke Students D,E,F	1:00 - 5:00 P.M. WPPC/Pt.Evaluations Students A,B,C	12:30 - 2:30 P.M. VietNam Vets PTSD Group w/Chaplain A.Todd and William Koruna, MSW VAMC Counseling Center Student D	1:30 - 5:00 P.M. VAMC Counseling Center w/Dr.Raval Student D	2:00 - 4:00 P.M. Clinical Seminar: "Transcultural Psychiatry -Papua New Guinea" Walter Turke, M.D. SCHI/MSU
1:00 - 4:00 P.M. WPPC w/Dr.Lovy Students A,B,C	1:00 - 5:00 P.M. VAMC Counseling Center w/Dr.Raval Student D	1:00 - 5:00 P.M. Consultation Liaison Psych w/Kaushik Raval, M.D. VAMC Counseling Center Students A,B,C	1:30 - 5:00 P.M. Psychodynamically Informed Psychopharm. Clinic w/Dr.Turke and 5:00 - 6:30 P.M. SCHI/MSU Group Therapy w/Dr.Turke Student A,B,C	[NOTE: Students' mid-term evaluations are due in Dr.Turke's MSU/SCHI office today.]
		* * * [DR.TURKE WILL BE IN EAST LANSING THIS AFTERNOON FOR MSU MEDICAL STUDENT EDUCATION COMM. MTG.] * * * *		

Student A-Angie Domingo, MSU III
Student B-Karen Jorgensen, MSU III
Student C-James Lieber, MSU III
Student D-Dominic Maxwell, MSU III
Student E-Thomas Ronay, MSU III
Student F-Allison Schwenda, MSU III

MSU/SCHI PSYCHIATRY CLERKSHIP REQUIRED SCHEDULE
SUMMER II TERM 1994
PAGE 5

SCHI - Dr. Turke's Office 771-6863
VAMC - Counseling Center 791-2242 or 793-2340, ex. 3730
CMH - Community Mental Health w/Dr.Lenhart 797-3400
SGH - Saginaw General Hospital M.H.U. 771-4250
WPPC - White Pine Psychiatric Center 790-7736
Dr. Lenhart's Private Practice Office 793-5303
Dr. Lovy's Office 790-7734

MONDAY, JULY 25

8:00 - 12:00 Noon	WPPC InPt. W/Dr.Lenhart Students A & B
8:00 - 12:00 Noon	Psych In-Takes w/Dr.Raval VAMC Counseling Center Students D,E,F
8:00 - 12:00 Noon	Delta Family Clinic w/Dr.Dutchak (684-9313) Student C
1:00 - 3:00 P.M.	SCHI/MSU Psychiatry Practice Center w/DrTurke and
3:00 - 4:30 P.M.	SCHI/MSU Group Therapy w/Dr.Turke Students A,B,C
1:00 - 4:00 P.M.	WPPC w/Dr.Lovy Students D,E,F

TUESDAY, JULY 26

8:30 - 10:30 A.M.	Clinical Seminar: "Anxiety Disorders" Walter Turke, M.D. SCHI/MSU Office
10:30 - 12:00 Noon	"Psychopharmacology of Anxiety Disorders" G.Robert DeYoung, Pharm D Saginaw Medical Center Lower Level, Room 430
1:00 - 5:00 P.M.	Community Mental Health w/Dr.Lenhart Students B & C
1:00 - 5:00 P.M.	WPPC/Pt.Evaluations Students D,E,F
1:00 - 5:00 P.M.	VAMC Counseling Center w/Dr.Raval Student A
6:00 - 9:00 P.M.	PSYCHIATRY CLUB Video: "Thelma & Louise" with Susan Sarandon and Geena Davis Dr.Turke's condo

WEDNESDAY, JULY 27

7:30 - 11:00 A.M.	VAMC Counseling Center w/Dr.Turke [Practice Exp]
12:00 - 5:00 P.M.	A.C.T. Program-Bay City w/Dr.Dutchak Student B
12:00 - 5:00 P.M.	A.C.T. Program-Saginaw w/Dr.Lenhart Studentd A & C
1:00 - 5:00 P.M.	Consultation Liaison Psych w/Kaushik Raval, M.D. VAMC Counseling Center Students D,E,F

THURSDAY, JULY 28

8:00 - 12:00 Noon	WPPC w/Dr.Lenhart Students A,B,C
8:00 - 12:00 Noon	WPPC w/Dr.Lovy Students D,E,F
1:00 - 5:00 P.M.	Community Mental Health w/Dr.Lenhart Students B & C
1:30 - 5:00 P.M.	Michigan Psych Assoc. w/Dr.Dutchak (895-2375) Student A
1:00 - 5:00 P.M.	Psychodynamically Informed Psychopharm. Clinic w/Dr.Turke and
5:00 - 6:30 P.M.	SCHI/MSU Group Therapy w/Dr.Turke Students D,E,F

FRIDAY, JULY 29

8:00 - 12:00 Noon	WPPC w/Dr.Lenhart Students A,B,C
8:00 - 12:00 Noon	WPPC w/Dr.Lovy Students D,E,F
1:00 - 2:00 P.M.	"Depression in Childhood" Faye Istanbooly, M.D. Saginaw Medical Center Lower Level, Room 430
2:30 - 3:00 P.M.	"E.C.T. Videotape" MSU Student Room

* * * [DR.TURKE IS ON VACATION TODAY] * * *

SATURDAY, JULY 30 & SUNDAY, JULY 31

7:30 - 10:00 A.M.	WPPC In-Patient Rounds Meet in Dr.Lovy's Office A234 A-Unit

Student A-Angie Domingo, MSU III
Student B-Karen Jorgensen, MSU III
Student C-James Lieber, MSU III
Student D-Dominic Maxwell, MSU III
Student E-Thomas Roney, MSU III
Student F-Allison Schwanda, MSU III

MSU/SCHI PSYCHIATRY CLERKSHIP REQUIRED SCHEDULE
SUMMER II TERM 1994
PAGE 6

SCHI - Dr. Turke's Office 771-6863
VAMC - Counseling Center 791-2242 or 793-2340, ex. 3730
CMH - Community Mental Health w/Dr.Lenhart 797-3400
SGH - Saginaw General Hospital M.H.U. 771-4250
WPPC - White Pine Psychiatric Center 790-7736
Dr. Lenhart's Private Practice Office 793-5303
Dr. Lovy's Office 790-7734

MONDAY, AUGUST 1	TUESDAY, AUGUST 2	WEDNESDAY, AUGUST 3	THURSDAY, AUGUST 4	FRIDAY, AUGUST 5
9:00 - 10:30 A.M. Tour of Caro Regional Mental Health Center 1-673-3191 (See directions in Orientation Book)	8:30 - 10:00 A.M. Clinical Seminar: "Delusions & Hallucinations" Walter Turke, M.D. SCHI/MSU Office	7:30 - 11:00 A.M. VAMC Counseling Center w/Dr.Turke [Practice Exp]	8:00 - 12:00 Noon WPPC w/Dr.Lenhart Students A & B	8:00 - 12:00 Noon WPPC w/Dr.Lenhart Students A & B
	10:00 - 11:00 A.M. "Neuropsychological Testing" Jan Caputo, Ph.D., Psy.D. Saginaw Medical Center Lower Level, Room 4100		8:00 - 12:00 Noon WPPC w/Dr.Lovy Students D & F	8:00 - 12:00 Noon WPPC w/Dr.Lovy Students D & F
		******************** [STUDENTS C & E PRESENTING AT AN OUT-OF-STATE CONFERENCE] ********************		
1:00 - 3:00 P.M. SCHI/MSU Psychiatry Practice Center w/DrTurke and	1:00 - 5:00 P.M. Community Mental Health w/Dr.Lenhart Students A & B	12:00 - 5:00 P.M. A.C.T. Program-Saginaw w/Dr.Lenhart Students A & B	1:00 - 5:00 P.M. Community Mental Health w/Dr.Lenhart Students A & B	2:00 - 4:00 P.M. Clinical Seminar: (Topic to be announced) Walter Turke, M.D. SCHI/MSU
3:00 - 4:30 P.M. SCHI/MSU Group Therapy w/Dr.Turke Students A,B,C	1:00 - 5:00 P.M. WPPC/Pt.Evaluations Students D,E,F	12:30 - 2:30 P.M. VietNam Vets PTSD Group w/Chaplain A.Todd and William Koruna, MSW VAMC Counseling Center Students D & F	1:30 - 5:00 P.M. Psychodynamically Informed Psychopharm. Clinic w/Dr.Turke Students D & F	
1:00 - 4:00 P.M. WPPC w/Dr.Lovy Students D,E,F	1:00 - 5:00 P.M. SCHI/MSU Psychiatry Practice Center w/DrTurke Student C		5:00 - 7:00 P.M. Dean's Office: Special Required Student Meeting	
********************	******************** [DR.RAVAL IS ON VACATION FROM AUGUST 1 THROUGH AUGUST 7] ********************			

Student A-Angie Domingo, MSU III
Student B-Karen Jorgensen, MSU III
Student C-James Lieber, MSU III
Student D-Dominic Maxwell, MSU III
Student E-Thomas Roney, MSU III
Student F-Allison Schwanda, MSU III

MSU/SCHI PSYCHIATRY CLERKSHIP REQUIRED SCHEDULE
SUMMER II TERM 1994
PAGE 7

SCHI - Dr. Turke's Office 771-6863
VAMC - Counseling Center 791-2242 or 793-2340, ex. 3730
CMH - Community Mental Health w/Dr.Lenhart 797-3400
SGH - Saginaw General Hospital M.H.U. 771-4250
WPPC - White Pine Psychiatric Center 790-7736
Dr. Lenhart's Private Practice Office 793-5303
Dr. Lovy's Office 790-7734

MONDAY, AUGUST 8	TUESDAY, AUGUST 9	WEDNESDAY, AUGUST 10	THURSDAY, AUGUST 11	FRIDAY, AUGUST 12
8:00 - 12:00 Noon WPPC InPt. W/Dr.Lenhart Students A & C 8:00 - 12:00 Noon Psych In-Takes w/Dr.Raval VAMC Counseling Center Students D,E,F 8:00 - 12:00 Noon Independent Study Student B	8:30 - 10:30 A.M. Clinical Seminar: "Gender Issues" Walter Turke, M.D. SCHI/MSU Office 11:00 - 12:00 Noon "Vincent Van Gogh" (Videotape) Walter Turke, M.D. SCHI/MSU Office	7:30 - 11:00 A.M. VAMC Counseling Center w/Dr.Turke [Practice Exp]	8:00 - 12:00 Noon WPPC w/Dr.Lenhart Students A,B,C 8:00 - 12:00 Noon WPPC w/Dr.Lovy Students D,E,F	8:00 - 12:00 Noon WPPC w/Dr.Lenhart Students A,B,C 8:00 - 12:00 Noon WPPC w/Dr.Lovy Students D,E,F
1:00 - 3:00 P.M. SCHI/MSU Psychiatry Practice Center w/DrTurke and 3:00 - 4:30 P.M. SCHI/MSU Group Therapy w/Dr.Turke Students A,B,C 1:00 - 4:00 P.M. WPPC w/Dr.Lovy Students D,E,F	1:00 - 5:00 P.M. Community Mental Health w/Dr.Lenhart Students A & C 1:00 - 5:00 P.M. WPPC/Pt.Evaluations Students D,E,F 1:00 - 5:00 P.M. VAMC Counseling Center w/Dr.Raval Student B 6:00 - 9:00 P.M. PSYCHIATRY CLUB Video: "The Life and Death of Malcolm X" Dr.Turke's condo	12:00 - 5:00 P.M. A.C.T. Program-Saginaw w/Dr.Lenhart Students A & C 12:30 - 2:30 P.M. VietNam Vets PTSD Group w/Chaplain A.Todd and William Koruna, MSW VAMC Counseling Center Student B 1:00 - 5:00 P.M. Consultation Liaison Psyc w/Kaushik Raval, M.D. VAMC Counseling Center Students D,E,F	1:00 - 5:00 P.M. Community Mental Health w/Dr.Lenhart Students A & C 1:00 - 5:00 P.M. VAMC Counseling Center w/Dr.Raval Student B 1:00 - 5:00 P.M. Psychodynamically Informed Psychopharm. Clinic w/Dr.Turke and 5:00 - 6:30 P.M. SCHI/MSU Group Therapy w/Dr.Turke Students D,E,F	1:00 - 2:30 P.M. "Coping with Losses" E.Kuschinsky, MSW Saginaw Medical Center Lower Level, Room 430 3:30 - 5:00 P.M. "Introduction to Schizophrenia" Kaushik Raval, M.D. VAMC Counseling Center * * * [DR.TURKE IS ON VACATION TODAY] * * *

Student A-Angie Domingo, MSU III
Student B-Karen Jorgensen, MSU III
Student C-James Lieber, MSU III
Student D-Dominic Maxwell, MSU III
Student E-Thomas Ronay, MSU III
Student F-Allison Schwanda, MSU III

MSU/SCHI PSYCHIATRY CLERKSHIP REQUIRED SCHEDULE
SUMMER II TERM 1994
PAGE 8

SCHI - Dr. Turke's Office 771-6863
VAMC - Counseling Center 791-2242 or 793-2340, ex. 3730
CMH - Community Mental Health w/Dr.Lenhart 797-3400
SGH - Saginaw General Hospital M.H.U. 771-4250
WPPC - White Pine Psychiatric Center 790-7736
Dr. Lenhart's Private Practice Office 793-5303
Dr. Lovy's Office 790-7734

MONDAY, AUGUST 15	TUESDAY, AUGUST 16	WEDNESDAY, AUGUST 17	THURSDAY, AUGUST 18	FRIDAY, AUGUST 19
8:00 - 12:00 Noon WPPC InPt. W/Dr.Lenhart Students B & C 8:00 - 12:00 Noon Psych In-Takes w/Dr.Raval VAMC Counseling Center Students D,E,F 8:00 - 12:00 Noon Independent Study Student A	8:30 - 10:30 A.M. Clinical Seminar: "Oral Quiz" Walter Turke, M.D. SCHI/MSU Office	7:30 - 11:00 A.M. VAMC Counseling Center w/Dr.Turke [Practice Exp]	8:00 - 12:00 Noon WPPC w/Dr.Lenhart Students A,B,C 8:00 - 12:00 Noon WPPC w/Dr.Lovy Students D,E,F	8:30 - 9:00 A.M. Students to complete Evaluation of Clerkship forms 9:00 - 11:00 A.M. FINAL EXAMINATION Saginaw Medical Center Lower Level, Room 430
1:00 - 3:00 P.M. SCHI/MSU Psychiatry Practice Center w/DrTurke and 3:00 - 4:30 P.M. SCHI/MSU Group Therapy w/Dr.Turke Students A,B,C 1:00 - 4:00 P.M. WPPC w/Dr.Lovy Students D,E,F	1:00 - 5:00 P.M. Community Mental Health w/Dr.Lenhart Students B & C 1:00 - 5:00 P.M. WPPC/Pt.Evaluations Students D,E,F 1:00 - 5:00 P.M. VAMC Counseling Center w/Dr.Raval Student A	12:00 - 5:00 P.M. A.C.T. Program-Saginaw w/Dr.Lenhart Students B & C 12:30 - 2:30 P.M. VietNam Vets PTSD Group w/Chaplain A.Todd and William Koruna, MSW VAMC Counseling Center Student A 1:00 - 5:00 P.M. Consultation Liaison Psych w/Kaushik Raval, M.D. VAMC Counseling Center Students D,E,F * * * [DR.TURKE WILL BE IN EAST LANSING THIS AFTERNOON FOR MSU MEDICAL STUDENT EDUCATION COMM. MTG.] * * * *	1:00 - 5:00 P.M. Independent Study All Students	**PLEASE NOTE: Students' comprehensive patient evaluation with psychodynamic formulation due in Dr.Turke's Office by 8:30 A.M., if not turned in earlier. Also, please return all clerkship materials prior to the exam, in addition to the six questions you need to write for future exams. [NOTE: Students' final evaluations are due in Dr.Turke's MSU/SCHI office today.]

Student A-Angie Domingo, MSU III
Student B-Karen Jorgensen, MSU III
Student C-James Lieber, MSU III
Student D-Dominic Maxwell, MSU III
Student E-Thomas Roney, MSU III
Student F-Allison Schwanda, MSU III

Representative Pictures of Students

Hayden Fry, Author, and Shirley Fry

Nobert Enzer, MSU Department of Psychiatry Chair, and Author

Essay on Cigars*

MICHIGAN STATE UNIVERSITY

COLLEGE OF HUMAN MEDICINE • SAGINAW CAMPUS
ASSISTANT DEAN (517) 771-6878
COMMUNITY ADMINISTRATOR (517) 771-6875

SAGINAW COOPERATIVE HOSPITALS
1000 HOUGHTON, SUITE 1000
SAGINAW • MICHIGAN • 48602

Department of Psychiatry (517) 771-6863

For Walter Turke, M.D., Cigar-Smoking Associate Professor of Psychiatry

<u>FOUR FREUDIAN & OTHER REASONS WHY MY HUSBAND IS "REPULSED"</u>

<u>BY MY NEW FRAGRANCE - EAU DE STALE CIGAR SMOKE</u>

by Dorene E. Jacobson, MSU III

1. The smell of stale cigar smoke may remind my husband that I've been spending more time with another man, and obviously have gotten close enough to that man to take on his own personal fragrance.

2. The smell of stale cigar smoke may represent the ability of another man to openly confront his latent homosexual tendencies by the public smoking of cigars, which are very phallic symbols. This may be stirring up certain homophobic feelings in my husband, who then projects these feelings onto his wife, who suddenly smells like a man!

3. Alternatively (or possibly in addition to), the smell of stale cigar smoke on his wife may remind my husband that his father used to smoke cigars, which led to both his mother and father smelling of the same. Thus, when smelling stale cigar smoke on his wife, my husband may be displacing his Oedipal feelings (and/or homosexual feelings towards his father) onto myself; everyone knows you should not make love to your mother (or your father!)!

4. Finally, my husband may simply be repulsed by the unpleasant ordor of stale cigar smoke!

P.S. Additional reasons should take into consideration both the oral and anal phases of life that the smoking of cigars can represent...(i.e., an oral fixation and/or the smoking of "little turds"). However, I feel that one, or possibly all four of the reasons listed above address the true reason(s) why my husband dislikes his wife coming home smelling of stale cigar smoke. (The combination of #2 and #3 is my personal favorite.)

*Used by permission.

Psychiatry Club Agenda

OF CANNIBAL FORKS AND SHRUNKEN HEADS: HOW TO KEEP A PSYCHIATRY CLUB GOING

WALTER TURKE, M.D., L.F.A.P.A.
ASSOCIATE PROFESSOR AND COORDINATOR, MEDICAL STUDENT CLERKSHIPS IN PSYCHIATRY, SAGINAW CAMPUS
DEPARTMENT OF PSYCHIATRY, COLLEGE OF HUMAN MEDICINE
MICHIGAN STATE UNIVERSITY

Psychiatry Club takes place at my condominium at Bay Valley Resort and occurs four times during the eight-week psychiatry clerkships. Attendance is required for students on Psychiatry, averaging 4-6 students, with whom I usually spend 150 hours while on the clerkship. All medical students on the Saginaw Campus receive written notice of each meeting and are invited to attend if they wish, registering with my administrative assistant.

Psychiatry Club usually meets Wednesdays at 6:00 P.M. and we furnish Pepsi and pizza. The 2300 square feet of my condo are covered with artifacts and momentos from world travels, such as a stone age axe and masks from Papua New Guinea, cannibal forks and warrior clubs from Fiji and a shrunken head from the Amazon Jungle with blow pipe and spears. These furnish the basis for discussion of transcultural issues and interesting stories. I also have a series of paintings from a university art professor who paid for his therapy by creating paintings about our relationship.

At times we view videotapes, interrupting the tape as needed to discuss psychodynamic observations. We choose videos that lend themselves to the latter, such as, "Thelma and Louise", "What About Bob?", "The Boys in the Band", and "Dressed to Kill". More recently we have begun to also add videos from the Black History Series on "Malcolm X", the films of Spike Lee, such as, "Jungle Fever" and "Do the Right Thing". I have also decided to pursue videos which are for sheer enjoyment such as "The Music Lovers", which is based on the life and music of Pyotr Ilyich Tchaikovsky, and also "Sophisticated Ladies" which is performed by the original Duke Ellington orchestra, conducted by Mercer Ellington, reliving the stage musical which highlighted 34 of the Duke's favorite songs. We also will spend an evening with Linda Ronstadt singing "Canciones de mi Padre" the former enhance rapport with our minority students, to facilitate the sharing of ideas, to provide cultural and ethnicity appreciation, and a pause from psychodynamics.

Learning Objectives: At the conclusion of the workshop the participants may have a better appreciation of how to conduct a Psychiatry Club and how to make the Psychiatry Clerkship "enjoyable" as well as meaningful.

Methods: Slides will be shown of my condo with representative samples of artifacts, paintings, and a few illustrative stories.

Appendix G
MSU A.B.L.E. Students

Press & Podium

Third-year MSU-CHM medical student **Allison Schwanda** is first author on an article titled "Brief Unconscious Sedation for Painful Pediatric Oncology Procedures: Intravenous Methohexital with Appropriate Monitoring is Safe and Effective". The article was published in the American Journal of Pediatric Hematology/Oncology 1993 Vol. 15 (4).

Robert W. Wolford, M.D., Director of Emergency Medicine, spoke January 26 at a meeting of the Downtown Rotary Club. Dr. Wolford, an Assistant Professor of Medicine at MSU-CHM, spoke on Emergency Medicine and its role in the Saginaw community.

Peter Vasilenko, Ph.D., Director of Research, and **Edward A. Jackson, M.D.,** Associate Director of Family Practice, submitted two abstracts to the American Diabetes Association for publication at its national meeting. The abstracts are titled "The Management and Outcome of Gestational Diabetes: Influence of Race and Payment Source" and "The Management of Gestational Diabetes by Family Physicians: Survey of Knowledge and Standards of Care"

Donald Passal, M.D., Director of Pediatrics, received the 1993 Distinguished Service Award from the Saginaw County Department of Public Health. This award is given to an individual who has made a contribution in the field of public health and to the overall health of the community.

Shirley Cresswell, BLD, Director of Laboratory Medicine, has been appointed to the Philippine Blood Coordinating Council. Ms. Cresswell also received a permanent appointment as Visiting Professor in the Department of Medicine and Surgery at the University of Santo Tomas, Manila. In addition, Ms. Cresswell is the co-author of two papers that were published in December in the University of Santo Tomas Journal and in the Journal of Philippine Society of Microbiology and Infectious Disease. One paper was on the detection of filariasis and the other was on the diagnosis of malaria by QBC.

Joseph F. Marshall, M.D., Director of Ob/Gyn, and **Peter Vasilenko, Ph.D.,** Director of Research, presented an update of the progress of the Saginaw County Infant Mortality Coalition at the National Conference on Fetal-Infant Mortality Review. The conference was on January 25-27 in Washington, D.C.

Radha Cherukuri, M.D., and **Daniel Wechter, M.D.,** Assistant Directors of Ob/Gyn and Co-Directors of the Division of Fetal-Maternal Medicine, attended the annual conference of the Society of Perinatal Obstetricians in Las Vegas, NV, during the week of January 24th.

Psychiatry Director A.B.L.E. to Help Minority Students

To increase the number of underrepresented minority students in the entering class of Michigan State University College of Human Medicine, the College created a program called A.B.L.E., or Advanced Baccalaureate Learning Experience. Walter Turke, M.D., Associate Professor of Psychiatry at MSU-CHM and Director of Psychiatry at S.C.H.I., serves as a psychiatry faculty representative to the A.B.L.E. Committee. The A.B.L.E. program is designed to provide a 13-month postbaccalaureate experience that allows students to enroll in selected first-year medical school courses and upper division undergraduate science courses. The program also provides small-group supplemental instruction, tutorials and continuous academic monitoring. Dr. Turke is hoping he can help students in the A.B.L.E. program, especially as the new CHM curriculum emphasizes more small group discussions and role playing.

"Minorities may not always do as well in those types of situations because they feel isolated," Dr. Turke said. "Past experience demonstrates that it is difficult for A.B.L.E. students to express their feelings and personal needs."

To help minority students feel more comfortable in small-group discussions, the committee of 14 faculty members and staff from the College of Human Medicine proposed a two-day retreat off campus following orientation sometime this spring. Dr. Turke offered the use of his condo and planned a program which includes sharing of his vulnerabilities, seminars on self-esteem and emotional wellness, videos with Afro-American and Mexican-American themes and men's and women's issues, and "survival hints." There will be ample time for camaraderie, recreation and relationship building. Dr. Turke will maintain ongoing contact with the students as they progress through the program.

Dr. Turke emphasized that the committee's recommendations still need to be reviewed and given approval by MSU Administration. As medical schools face economically trying times, resources provided for special programs for students at risk are likely to raise concerns. However, the A.B.L.E. program is driven by MSU's humanistic values and is receiving strong support from the Dean and College. "The A.B.L.E. program will aid in serving in medically underserved areas in the state of Michigan," Dr. Turke said. "In addition, the students will serve as role models for their peers."

MICHIGAN STATE
UNIVERSITY

A.B.L.E. STUDENTS' RETREAT
June 25-26, 1994

SATURDAY, JUNE 25

10:00 AM ARRIVAL - Dr. Walter Turke's condominium, 6289 Golf Lakes Court B, Bay City (517) 686-0003, Soft Drinks, Introductions, Tour of Dr. Turke's condo with discussion of world travel artifacts as "icebreaker"

11:00 AM SEMINAR: "Emotional Wellness for Medical Students & Physicians" Walter Turke, M.D., Associate Professor of Psychiatry, CHM/MSU

12:30 PM COOKOUT - Hamburgers, Hot Dogs, etc.

2:00 PM NATURE WALK to Delta College and back

3:00 PM GROUP SHARING - Initiated by Walter Turke sharing his vulnerabilities; growing up with low self-esteem in poverty with immigrant parents in Brooklyn, New York

5:00 PM DINNER - Pepsi, Pizza at condo with music by Los Lobos, Linda Ronstadt, Billie Holiday, and Duke Ellington

6:30 PM VIDEO: "500 Years of Resistance", Herminia Garcia Ortega, M.A., Educational Development Specialist, CHM/MSU

7:30 PM GROUP SHARING -- A.B.L.E. Students

8:30 PM VIDEO: "The Life and Death of Malcolm X"

10:30 PM ADJOURNMENT to Best Western Saginaw, 3325 Davenport Avenue, (517) 793-2080 rooms are guaranteed for late arrival in Dr. Turke's name.

SUNDAY, JUNE 26

8:30 AM BREAKFAST at Best Western Saginaw

10:00 AM VIDEO: "Eyes on the Prize" - Martin Luther King Julianne Price, ABLE Program Coordinator, CHM/MSU

11:30 AM SUNDAY BRUNCH at Bay Valley Resort (Casual Dress Acceptable)

1:00 PM MULTICULTURAL SHARING: "Papua New Guinea Odyessy", Dr. Turke

3:00 PM ADJOURNMENT - Arrange for regular follow-up interactions with A.B.L.E. Students and Dr. Turke

COLLEGE OF
HUMAN MEDICINE
Office of the Assistant Dean for Saginaw
Saginaw Cooperative Hospitals, Inc.
1000 Houghton Avenue
Suite 1000
Saginaw, Michigan
48602
517/771-6878
FAX 517/753-3439

'94 A.B.L.E. STUDENTS RETREAT

Thanks for everything
Dr. Turke. Your kindness
will always be remembered
Sincerely,
Chiqui Simpkins

Thank for everything
[illegible]

Dr. Turke,
I enjoyed myself
at your retreat. Thank
You Very Much!!
Charles Black
P.S. Maybe we can
DO IT AGAIN.

Dr. Turke,
I enjoyed your company, information,
and hospitality. The weekend made
a huge difference in the continuity
of the group. Thanks for your
Generosity!!
Titus Vergeh

Thanks
Dr. Turke
It was real-
Samuel Adams

Thank you for everything
God bless you
Sincerely
Veronica

Thank you
Dr. Turke, I appreciate
everything you
have done and the
weekend. It
was quite
helpful!
[illegible]

Dr. Turke,
Thanks for the tour of
your museum. I learned
a lot. Your generosity
is deeply appreciated.
You have shared something
with me that will last a
lifetime. Thanks Again, Nora Land

Thank you
for opening your
home to us and
thank you for
the insights on your
travels and the
world of psychiatry.
S. [illegible]

Thank you for the
wonderful weekend
Arlette
Chambers

Appendix H
Excellence in Clinical Teaching Award 1993

Certificate of Excellence in Teaching

awarded to

Walter Turke, M.D.

Presented as a token of sincere appreciation and recognition of your dedication, interest in, and support to minority students at the College.

Minority Medical Student Association
Graduating Class of 1993
College of Human Medicine
Michigan State University

Excellence in Clinical Teaching Award
Graduating Seniors 1995

CERTIFICATE OF EXCELLENCE
IN TEACHING

Walter Turke, M.D.

Presented as a token of sincere appreciation and recognition of your dedication, interest, and ability in the art of teaching.

The Class of 1995
College of Human Medicine
Michigan State University

Appendix I

Excellence in Clinical Teaching Award 1994

Certificate of Excellence in Teaching

awarded to

Walter Turke, M.D.

Presented as a token of sincere appreciation and recognition of your dedication, interest in, and support to minority students at the College.

Minority Medical Student Association
Graduating Class of 1994
College of Human Medicine
Michigan State University

Appendix J

Spirituality and Human Values in Medicine Conference Schedule

CHRONOLOGICAL LISTING OF
SPIRITUALITY AND HUMAN VALUES IN MEDICINE CONFERENCES

SAGINAW COOPERATIVE HOSPITALS, INC.
(SHVIM)

MAY 16, 1989	"SUFFERING AND PAIN", SMC Moderator: Barbara J. Sucher, MBA Entire Committee participated
SEPTEMBER 27, 1989	"THE MANY FACES OF HATRED: THE ISMS", SMC (RACISM, SEXISM, ETC.) Moderator: Guest Speakers: Howard Brody, M.D., Marian R. Purdue, MSN Donna Long
NOVEMBER 15, 1989	"SAFE PASSAGE TO DEATH", SLHC Moderator: Guest Speakers: Walter Turke, M.D. Mary Schuetz Kathryn Trier, B.S.N., M.S.
JANUARY 24, 1990	"SEXUALITY AND SPIRITUALITY: KISSING COUSINS", SMC Moderator: Guest Speakers: Beth Alexander, M.D. Terry Stein, M.D. Perry Engstrom, MSW
MARCH 28, 1990	"THE PERPLEXING PARADOX OF GUILT", SMC Moderator: David C. Engstrom, M.D. Guest Speaker: John M. Schneider, Ph.D.
SEPTEMBER 12, 1990	"EMOTIONAL WELLNESS OF THE HEALTH CARE GIVER", SMC Moderator: Robert D. Leas, M.Div. Guest Speakers: Walter Turke, M.D. and Robert D. Leas, M.Div.
NOVEMBER 14, 1990	"FORGIVENESS", SMC Moderator: John P. Foglio, D.Min. Guest Speaker: John M. Schneider, Ph.D.
FEBRUARY 26, 1991	"IDEALISM IN MEDICINE...FACT OR FICTION?" Moderator: Barbara J. Sucher, MBA Guest Speaker: Daniel S. Mazzuchi, M.D.
MAY 8, 1991	"MID-LIFE CRISIS", SMC Moderator: David Engstrom, M.D. Guest Speaker: Norbert Enzer, M.D.
SEPTEMBER 18, 1991	"THE MEANING OF HEALING", SMC Co-Moderators: Walter Turke, M.D. and Robert D. Leas, M.Div. Guest Speaker: Co-Moderators
NOVEMBER 20, 1991	"FEAR OF INTIMACY", SMC Moderator: John P. Foglio, D.Min. Guest Speaker: Joan Jackson Johnson, Ph.D.

JANUARY 15, 1992	"SPIRITUALITY AND HOLISM", SMC Moderator: John P. Foglio, D.Min. Guest Speaker: Bishop Kenneth Untener
MARCH 25, 1992	"LIFE STORIES OF PERSONS 'AFFECTED' BY THE AIDS VIRUS" Moderator: Barbara J. Sucher, MBA Guest Speaker: Martha Jenson, M.D.
NOVEMBER 18, 1992	"FAMILY VIOLENCE", SMC Moderator: David C. Engstrom, M.D. Guest Speaker: Linda Schmidt, Underground Railroad
JANUARY 20, 1993	POSTPONEMENT: "AVOIDANCE OF INTIMACY IN THE CARE PROVIDER'S MARRIAGE" Moderator: Robert D. Leas, M.Div. Guest Speaker: Arnold Werner, M.D., MSU-CHM
MARCH 30, 1993	"STARRY, STARRY NIGHT" - *A Birthday Tribute to Vincent from His Friend, Walter* Moderator and Speaker: Walter Turke, M.D.
MAY 26, 1993	"THE 'WISE' PHYSICIAN" Co-Moderators: Barbara J. Sucher, MBA and John P. Foglio, D.Min. Speaker: Father James J. Gill
SEPTEMBER 15, 1993	"Setting Limits" Moderator: David C. Engstrom, M.D.
November 17, 1993	"Hope vs Despair: Can Hope Survive?" Co-Moderators: W. Turke, M.D. and J. Foglio, D.Min.
January 19, 1994	"Tyranny of Dependency" Moderator: Robert D. Leas, M.Div.

Appendix K
World Travel List of Walter Turke, M.D.

TRAVELS**
1938 Germany
1965 Canada: Eastern, Central, Western
1966 Hawaiian Islands: Oahu, Hawaii, Maui, Kauai
1967 Mexico: Yucatan Peninsula and Cozumel
1968 Europe: Denmark, Holland, Germany, Switzerland and Hungary
1969 Orient: Japan, Hong Kong, Malaysia, Singapore, Macao, and Thailand
1970 Soviet Union and Greece
1971 Isle Royale, Lake Superior, Michigan
1977 Egypt and England
1978 Caribbean Sea: Puerto Rico and Virgin Islands
1979 Africa: Morocco and Kenya
1980 South America: Peru, Ecuador and Amazon Jungle
1980 People's Republic of China, Hong Kong and Philippine Islands
1984 South Pacific: Tahiti, Bora Bora, Moorea, New Zealand, Australia, Papua New Guinea and Fiji
1987 South America: Argentina, Brazil, Uruguay, Paraguay
1988 West Africa: Dakar, Senegal
1993 South Caribbean Sea: Barbados, Mayreau, Marinique, St. Martin, St. Thomas, San Juan
1993 Greece: Athens, Rhodes, Crete; Turkey: Istanbul, Ephesus; Limassol, Cyprus; Israel: Jerusalem, Bethlehem; Italy: Naples, Sorrento, Pompei, Rome

** (Knowledge used to incorporate transcultural issues with appreciation of diversity, in all its parameters, including minority concerns.)

1/95

Letters from Hayden Fry, University of Iowa Head Football Coach

IOWA FOOTBALL

Iowa Football
The University of Iowa
114 Recreation Building
Iowa City, Iowa 52242-1186

(319) 335-8944

1981 Big Ten Champions
1982 Rose Bowl
1982 Peach Bowl
1983 Gator Bowl
1984 Freedom Bowl
1985 Big Ten Champions
1986 Rose Bowl
1986 Holiday Bowl
1987 Holiday Bowl
1988 Peach Bowl
1990 Big Ten Champions
1991 Rose Bowl
1991 Holiday Bowl

March 10, 1993

Walter Turke, M.D.
Associate Professor of Psychiatry
Michigan State University - Saginaw Campus
1000 Houghton Avenue
Saginaw, MI 48602

Dear Walter:

I truly enjoyed visiting with you on the Hawkeye Cruise. Everyone was most complimentary of you and marveled at the fact that a MSU man could be so much fun.

Thanks also for the staff photo. You have surrounded yourself with some winners!

Hope to see you this spring.

Warm regards,

Hayden

Hayden Fry
Head Football Coach

HF:rf

IOWA FOOTBALL

Iowa Football
The University of Iowa
114 Recreation Building
Iowa City, Iowa 52242-1186

(319) 335-8944

1981 Big Ten Champions
1982 Rose Bowl
1982 Peach Bowl
1983 Gator Bowl
1984 Freedom Bowl
1985 Big Ten Champions
1986 Rose Bowl
1986 Holiday Bowl
1987 Holiday Bowl
1988 Peach Bowl
1990 Big Ten Champions
1991 Rose Bowl
1991 Holiday Bowl

May 13, 1993

Walter Turke, M.D.

Dear Walter:

All of the coaches and their wives join me in expressing our sincere appreciation to you for helping make Hawkeye Cruise VII such an enjoyable experience. We are already excited about the plans for next year's cruise.

Please accept the enclosed t-shirt as a memento of the wonderful time we spent together. Hope to see you on board next year.

Warm personal regards,

Hayden

Hayden Fry
Head Football Coach

HF:dj

Enc.

THE UNIVERSITY OF IOWA

Iowa Coach Hayden Fry ranks fourth among all Division I active coaches, beginning the 1993 season with 194 career victories. Fry is in his 15th season as the Hawkeye head coach.

IOWA FOOTBALL

December 7, 1993

Dear Walter:

Thank you for the nice note regarding my 200th victory. It would not have been possible had it not been for the wonderful support of the Iowa fans and for the great assistance of my staff, coaches and players over the years. I will always treasure your loyalty and friendship.

I'm looking forward to meeting your daughter and son-in-law on the Hawkeye cruise.

Sincerely,

Hayden Fry
Head Football Coach

HF:jd

IOWA FOOTBALL

Hayden Fry
Head Coach

March 7, 1995

Dr. Walter Turke
Bay Valley Resort
6289 Golf Lakes Court
Bay City, MI 48706

Dear Walter:

What a beautiful surprise to receive the birthday card. I am saddened to learn of your prostate problem, but happy to know that you went directly to the source of your problems.

I am confident you will be with all of the great Hawkeye fans on our cruise next February.

Walter, keep the faith. You are a winner and we love you.

God Bless!

Hayden

Hayden Fry
Head Football Coach

HF:km

The University of Iowa 114 Recreation Building Iowa City, Iowa 52242-1186 (319) 335-8944 FAx (319) 335-8915

I O W A F O O T B A L L

Hayden Fry
Head Coach

May 15, 1995

Walter Turke, M.D.
6289 Golf Lakes Court
Bay Valley Resort
Bay City, MI 48706

Dear Walter:

I am extremely happy to know that you will once again be with us on our Hawkeye Cruise next February. It will be our tenth consecutive cruise in the Caribbean and touted as one of the best of all time. Your presence will help assure that prediction.

Congratulations on your book! I'm confident that it will become a best seller. I don't recall what I said in my letters to you but you certainly have my permission to include whatever you desire in your book. I greatly value your friendship and admire the professional work you do to help your students and patients. Enjoy the spring!

Sincerely,

Hayden

Hayden Fry
Head Football Coach

HF:rf

I O W A

Hayden Fry
Head Coach

September 22, 1995

Walter Turke, M.D.
Michigan State University
College of Human Medicine
1000 Houghton, Suite 1000
Saginaw, MI 48602

Dear Walter:

It's always great to receive your note of good wishes.

The Hawks join me in thanking you for your continued support, and we wish you an enjoyable fall. On Iowa! Go Hawks! Beat MSU!

Sincerely,

Hayden

Hayden Fry
Head Football Coach

HF:rf

The University of Iowa 114 Recreation Building Iowa City, Iowa 52242-1186 (319) 335-8944 FAx (319) 335-8915

Appendix L

Newspaper Article—Religion

RELIGION

Sometimes you have to say no

Pastors need strategy to cope with pressures of parishioners

BY DENISE FORD-MITCHELL
News Staff Writer

News Staff/ Bernie Eng

Dr. Walter Turke, director of psychiatry at Saginaw Cooperative Hospitals Inc., 1000 Houghton, discusses ways that clergy and their spouses can cope with stress.

On call is a way of life, say many Saginaw County ministers.

"Although we frequently go that extra mile to console others, we somehow think it's healthy to neglect our own humanity," said the Rev. Robert Eggers, a pastor at Peace Lutheran Church, 3427 Adams.

"Even God took the seventh day to rest. But we, as ministers, tend to think we are some type of ecclesiastical Duracell battery that can go on and on and on."

There are other ways for pastors to cope with the demands and pressures of their profession, said Dr. Walter Turke, a Michigan State University associate psychiatry professor and director of psychiatry at Saginaw Cooperative Hospitals Inc., 1000 Houghton.

The first step, he explained, is for ministers to honestly assess their "emotional wellness."

"Clergy shepherd their flock, frequently at the expense of their own emotional health and well-being," said Turke at a recent "Emotional Well-Being for Clergy" conference for ministers and their spouses in Saginaw.

"Trying to please everyone is a common mistake many ministers make. For some pastors it is easier to help others than to help themselves.

"The characteristics of people called to the ministry compounds the problem because their acceptance of self is sometimes not developed enough to help them set appropriate boundaries," Turke said.

As many as 20 percent of America's 300,000-plus full-time clergy suffer long-term stress, according to a report in the Nov. 23, 1992, issue of Christianity Today.

And in 1989, the Southern Baptist Convention shelled out $64 million in medical benefits for pastors. Of those, stress-related claims ranked second.

"Being all things to all people is an impossible and stress-riddled task. The expectations others have of their spiritual leaders is absurd at times. No wonder the clergy are stressed.

"The church members expect the pastor to be the role model, the loving mother/father they never had and the person who knows everything about everything, which are impossible tasks," Turke emphasized.

In a 1984 study of 300 Protestant pastors, 70 percent said they do not have a close friend.

Ninety percent reported working more than 45 hours per week. Most stated their work week comes closer to 60-plus hours – and nearly 80 percent believe their ministry has adversely affected their families.

In that same study one-half of the respondents felt unable to meet the needs of their job, while 90 percent said they were inadequately trained to cope with the demands of pastoral ministry.

"A pastor in the average parish, especially one with a school, is called in so many directions – school, adults, children, hospital, ministry, funerals, weekly preaching.

"It can be particularly frustrating when there are five to six crises happening at the same time, which drains ministers' emotional resources significantly," Turke said.

"Parishioners tend to feel their needs come first and that the families of clergy are so spiritual and giving that other people's needs come first."

Pastors have a moral obligation to confront their congregation "in a very real way."

The down side, however, is outspoken ministers risk angering those who sit on church committees and pay their salaries, he said.

However, there are steps clergy can take to help reduce the stress of working round the clock, Turke said.

He suggests:

- Scheduling shorter or rotating holiday services so ministers can spend more time with their families.
- Reducing the number of worship services and activities. "Two ministers can not do the work of three and one can not do the work of two. And the maximum time period for services should be 60 minutes. Everything that needs to be said can be covered in one hour," Turke said.
- Sending out an annual schedule, noting which days they are not available to perform weddings or funerals.
- Maintaining a 40- to 50-hour work week, including church services.
- Compensating with time off when work extends beyond 50 hours.
- Taking two days off a week.
- Delegating and referring some of the work load to others.
- Limiting phone calls to working hours.
- Using answering machines at home.
- Stopping "drop-ins" at night. "Some 'emergencies' can wait until the next day," Turke said.
- Learning how to say "no." "Let parishioners know you have prior commitments," Turke said.

'It's important for church members to remember clergy have spouses and children who need nurturing, as do the clergy."

MSU Awards

CERTIFICATE OF APPRECIATION

awarded to

Walter Turke, M.D.

For Outstanding and Dedicated Service

Minority Medical Student Association
Graduating Class of 1995
College of Human Medicine
Michigan State University

Appendix M
Intro to College of Human Medicine, MSU

MICHIGAN STATE
UNIVERSITY

March 29, 1995

Dr. Walter Turke
1000 Houghton Avenue
Saginaw, MI 48602

Dear Dr. Turke:

Greetings to you from the College of Human Medicine.

As you may know, it gives us great pleasure to personally inform you that our medical school has been selected as the third best medical school in the nation for the education and training of primary care physicians by *U.S. News & World Report.* This achievement is highlighted in the March 20 issue of the magazine, available on newsstands now.

CHM's appearance in the magazine's annual survey of America's best graduate schools marks the 5th consecutive year in which the College has been ranked in the top 20. This most recent ranking is the College's highest since 1991, when it tied for 3rd.

U.S. News & World Report evaluated medical schools within two categories: research-oriented and primary care. The latter category reflects the 62 medical schools that graduated the highest share of M.D.'s who entered the primary care specialties of family practice, general internal medicine and pediatrics. Other indices used in the survey included student selectivity, faculty resources, and primary care rate. Twenty percent of the weighted score was based on peer evaluation of reputation as valued by medical school deans, senior faculty and directors of intern-residency programs.

National rankings like this have many effects on the medical school. Certainly, it builds pride amongst alumni, faculty, students and residents. Prospective applicants are interested in these rankings, and we can assuredly predict that applications at CHM will continue on an upward spiral again next year. Most importantly, it gives us national recognition for something we have known for a long time...that Michigan State University's College of Human Medicine has an extraordinary cadre of faculty -- both in East Lansing and in the community campuses -- whose commitment assures the excellence of our program and the high level of preparedness of our students. Thus, in a very real measure, the national ranking received by the College is a most-deserving affirmation of you and a real validation of your efforts.

On behalf of the College of Human Medicine, we proudly acknowledge you for your dedication and outstanding service to students, the College, your community, and the people of Michigan. Thank you for the significant role you personally have played in building the College's reputation.

Sincerely,

William S. Abbett
Dean

David Engstrom, M.D.
President, Saginaw Cooperative Hospital, Inc.
Assistant Dean CHM/Saginaw Campus

COLLEGE OF
HUMAN MEDICINE

Office of the Dean

East Fee Hall
East Lansing, Michigan
48824-1316

517/353-1730
FAX 517/355-0342